D1568316

PRAYING THE
GOSPELS

MATHEW, MARK, LUKE, AND JOHN

PRAYING THE

GOSPELS

MATHEW, MARK, LUKE, AND JOHN

Book Five in the Series
Praying the Scriptures

Elmer L. Towns

Destiny Image® Publishers, Inc.
P.O. Box 310
Shippensburg, PA 17257-0310

*"Speaking to the Purposes of God for this Generation
and for the Generations to Come."*

For Worldwide Distribution, Printed in the U.S.A.

ISBN 13: 978-0-7684-2439-3

This book and all other Destiny Image, Revival Press, MercyPlace, Fresh Bread, Destiny Image Fiction, and Treasure House books are available at Christian bookstores and distributors worldwide.

1 2 3 4 5 6 7 8 9 10 11 / 09 08 07

For a U.S. bookstore nearest you, call
1-800-722-6774.

For more information on foreign distributors, call
717-532-3040.

Or reach us on the Internet:
www.destinyimage.com

CONTENTS

INTRODUCTION

When you pray your way through the life of Jesus Christ, you are just about as close to the Father as you can get; because Jesus and the Father are One (see John 10:30). So try to live what you learn in this book as you pray your way through it.

This is the fifth book I've written in the series, *Praying the Scriptures*. I've followed the same format in each—I *translated* the passage from the original Greek into modern language. But it's not a word-for-word translation; rather it's a thought-for-thought edition. The second step is to *transliterate* the passage into the second person of English grammar. That was easy in Psalms where every verse was transliterated into a prayer. But in the Gospels, it's hard to do. There are a lot of descriptions of events so I've added a prayer at the beginning or end of these events, and sometimes I drop a prayer right in the middle of the events.

What you're holding in your hands is a paraphrase of the Scriptures so I encourage you to compare each section with the Bible references you'll find there.

When I first began this series of *Praying the Scriptures* I added a lot of information about the author, background, or difficult areas to interpret. But I changed my strategy in *Praying the Gospels*. In this book I've included stories to give you background to explain the culture and religious practices of that day. These stories were taken from an earlier book I wrote (*The Son*, Regal Books, 1999; and can be read free at www.elmertowns.com), and in some cases, the story was taken from a condensation of the events in *Guideposts Condensed Books, The Son* (Carmel, NY: Guideposts, pages 194-301).

There are four Gospels, each one telling stories about Jesus from a different perspective. Rather than praying through all four Gospels, I've translated them into one story but I've included bits and pieces from the other Gospels so you have a complete story. When you pray through one event in Jesus' life, you're exposed to all the Gospels.

When you read the Bible, you fill your head (intellect) with biblical material, but the content may not reach the heart (emotions) and you don't do what the Bible tells you (will). But when you *Pray the Scriptures*, you engage all three aspects of personality—intellect, emotion, and will. Obviously you're reading the Scriptures to pray them, so your *mind* is engaged. Then your *emotions* are involved because you're praying for God to help you understand the message. And when you ask God to let the truth of Scripture flow into your life—you've engaged your *will*. So, *Praying the Scriptures* may do much more for you than just reading your Bible. Allow God to change you through this reading experience.

My prayer is that when you are *Praying the Gospels* you will touch God, and put yourself in a position where God may touch you. If that happens, then the purpose of this book is fulfilled.

Sincerely yours in Christ,
Elmer L. Towns
Written from my home at the foot of the Blue Ridge Mountains
Summer 2006

Part One

JESUS—IMMANUEL

Chapter 1

THE GOSPEL OF LUKE

Luke 1:1-4

While Paul was in prison in Caesarea, Luke wrote a biography of Jesus and addressed it to a rich Christian named Theophilus (his name means "lover of wisdom"). A church probably met in Theophilus' house, and since he was rich, he probably had a library where he kept books for casual reading or serious study. Probably some Christian manuscripts were kept there also. Most wealthy men had an educated slave who could copy manuscripts for his master. Perhaps Theophilus had sent his slave to copy some of Paul's letters, to places like Colosse (the Book of Colossians) and Ephesus (the Book of Ephesians) and Galatia (the Book of Galatians).

Theophilus probably sent money to pay for Paul's expenses while he was in prison. In return, Luke sent Theophilus a complete biography of the life and works of Jesus, and explained, *"I have interviewed original eyewitnesses of the life of Christ, so I could write a complete narrative giving accurate information about the life of Christ"* (Luke 1:2,3 ELT). Luke also read all the bits and pieces of stories about Jesus and used them as sources for his biography of Jesus, *"Many have undertaken the task of writing the things we believe about Jesus...I in turn have gone over the whole course of their description..."* (Luke 1:1,3 ELT).

Like a newspaper reporter gathering all the facts before writing a story, Luke did his research in books and interviews (he did his research and writing while Paul was two years in prison). As Luke began to write, it was not the usual process of writing. Luke was inspired by the Holy Spirit so that what he wrote was accurate and without error. Luke was even aware of what was happening because he said, *"It seemed good to me also, having had perfect understanding*

11

of all things from above…" (Luke 1:3 ELT). The phrase "from above" is *anothen* in the original Greek which also means "from the very first." Luke testified he had perfect understanding from above—from God. The Gospel of Luke is the authority of God because he wrote what God told him to write, and he did it with the inspirational help of God.

Introduction to Luke

Luke 1:1-4

Lord, Luke said that many others have written a biography
 Of the events of Jesus on the earth;
He researched carefully the reports they wrote
 And he interviewed disciples who followed Him,
 And eyewitnesses who saw these things.
So that he would have perfect understanding
 To write an accurate account of Jesus,
Luke wrote the events in perfect sequence,
 Being inspired by God from on high.
Therefore, Theophilus had confidence in
 The things that have been taught to him.

Lord, I have confidence in the things
 That have been taught to me from Your Word,
 And I will study it carefully to know what You said.

Chapter 2

AN ANGEL SPEAKS

The Story of God Promising Zechariah a Son

Luke 1:5-25

The old man looked wistfully to the distant mountains. The leathery skin stretched over his frail bones told that he was past 60 years of age. He looked for Messiah to come each day; the One who would deliver his people from Rome's oppression. But the Messiah had not come.

"Come inside to eat," said his elderly wife who stood at the door of their home in Abia, a community that was home to Jerusalem's priests.

"I'm not hungry."

His wife asked, "Not hungry? Is it because of joy...or sadness?"

Zechariah smiled. Tomorrow would be his last day of temple duty. He was retiring. Tomorrow, when he entered the Holy Room to offer evening prayers, it would be his first and last time to pray for his nation. Priestly duties were assigned by lottery, and a priest could have the privilege of burning incense in the Holy Place usually once in his lifetime—sometimes never. If the selection had not been made for tomorrow, Zechariah would have ended his service unfulfilled.

"Don't frown," his wife, Elizabeth, told Zechariah. "You'll do fine."

Zechariah was not worried about praying.

"I'm concerned about the younger priests," he told his wife. "They do not love people, they love power. They have lost their faith."

"And why not?" Elizabeth wondered. "What is there to have faith in?"

13

"Hush!" Zechariah protested. "We must have faith in the Word of God; we must not look for miracles."

"I do. I do," Elizabeth declared. "But where is God? If the Almighty One loves His people, why doesn't He send Messiah to drive the Romans into the sea?"

The next day, excitement swept Zechariah and Elizabeth along the path on their short walk to Jerusalem. Friends and family accompanied them.

They entered the temple and Zechariah reached out to rub the gold on its gate one last time in his official role as a priest. Inside he glimpsed the 12 golden stairs and on a platform the Levitical choir.

Behind the choir were 12 more golden stairs. Clusters of people milled about, beginning to fill the large courtyards of the temple.

The priest in the pinnacle measured the falling shadow on the sundial, and when it was four o'clock, he put a trumpet to his lips and sounded the call for prayers. When the last note finished, the choir began to sing.

Zechariah climbed the golden stairs toward the Holy Room. Supportive eyes watched him disappear between its heavy curtains.

Zechariah stood before the Lord. He bowed his head in gratitude. I'm going to pray for myself, before I pray for Israel, he thought. "*Lord…give me a son.*"

He didn't mean to ask for a child—he blurted out the words without thinking. It was a prayer he had uttered many times. Elizabeth, his wife, was barren. Thousands of times he had asked for a son.

A cold shiver ran down Zechariah's back. There before him was a beautiful young man. He scared Zechariah because no one was supposed to be in the Holy Room except the appointed priest.

"Fear not," the young man said. "I am Gabriel. God wants you to know your prayers have been heard. Your wife will become pregnant and deliver a son."

"No!" the old priest protested. "We are too old for children."

"Your son will be special," Gabriel continued. "He will announce the Deliverer of Israel."

"The Messiah is coming?" Zechariah's eyes lit up.

"Your son will not be Messiah," the angel explained, "but your son will prepare the people for His coming."

"But I'm too old," Zechariah protested again.

Gabriel paid no attention. "Your son will have the name John," he instructed.

"Can you prove this?" Zechariah sputtered. "How will I know?"

"Because you did not believe the words of God, you will be unable to speak until the child is born." Gabriel pointed with an outstretched finger to Zechariah's mouth.

"Ugh...ugh...ugh...." Nothing came out of Zechariah's mouth.

"*Forgive me...forgive me*," Zechariah prayed silently. Then the old man crumpled to the floor.

The crowd of worshipers outside was becoming restless. Zechariah had been in the Holy Place much longer than was usual. The other priests knew they couldn't enter the Holy Room to see what was wrong, but they had to do something. The sun was setting, and the blessing hadn't been given.

One priest spoke to quiet the crowd. "Be patient...he will come out soon."

The curtains rippled. Zechariah stepped out onto the stairs. "Give the benediction!" one of the clerics called.

Zechariah shook his head and pointed to his mouth. "Ugh...ugh...ugh..." were the only sounds he could make.

The archpriest, sensing trouble, stepped beside his old friend. Lifting his hand, he said to the people, "The Lord bless and keep you. The Lord make His face to shine upon you. The Lord lift up His countenance upon you and give you peace."

My Time To Pray

- Lord, help me to wait patiently for the events in life when I will be the most effective for you.

- Help me to be sensitive to Your inner voice when You are trying to guide my life.

- Lord, sometimes I don't believe Your Word just as Zechariah didn't believe You. Help me to see my unbelief and give me a trusting heart.

- Lord, may I be quick to act on Your promises, something Zechariah didn't do.

- Lord, I want my personal life to honor You and I want to be faithful in service to the end of my life, as was Zechariah.

God Promises Zechariah a Son

Luke 1:5-25

Lord, Luke began to describe the events
    During the reign of King Herod.
Zechariah, a priest of the Abijah corps,
    Had married Elizabeth who was from the priestly family,
    So he had impeccable qualifications to serve God.
Zechariah and Elizabeth were spiritually minded
    And they carefully obeyed every aspect of religious law,
    And because Elizabeth was barren, they had no children.
When it finally came Zechariah's turn to offer
    Evening prayers in the Holy Place for all Israel,
He also entered to burn incense,

A symbol of prayers ascending up to God.
A great multitude was outside praying
At the tenth hour, which was 4 P.M.

Lord, may I be as faithful to You
As were Zechariah and Elizabeth in all things.

Lord, the appearance of an angel standing by the altar of incense
Frightened Zechariah;
The angel said, "Do not be afraid,
God has heard your prayers,
Your wife Elizabeth will have a son
And you must name him John."
"Your son will give you joy and happiness
And multitudes will rejoice with you."

Lord, help me receive Your message
When You come to speak to me.

Lord, the angel told Zechariah, "Your son will be a great man for God,
He must never drink intoxicating liquor,
And the Holy Spirit will fill him for service.
"Your son will convince many to turn to God,
He will be rugged like Elijah
And will precede the coming Deliverer.
"He will prepare for the coming of Deliverer
By softening the hearts of fathers to be like children,
And convincing the disobedient to return to Your wisdom."
Zechariah objected saying he was an old man,
And his wife was beyond child-bearing years.

Lord, when You promise to work in my life
May I never disbelieve Your Word.

The angel Gabriel reminded Zechariah that
He heard this good news standing in the presence of God,

And that God sent him to tell Zechariah.
Because Zechariah didn't believe God would do the things
    For which he prayed all his life,
Then the angel said that Zechariah wouldn't be able to speak
    Until the child was born.

Lord, may I be quick to believe, quick to
    Obey all You tell me to do.

The waiting crowd got anxious because Zechariah tarried
    And he couldn't speak when he appeared,
    So they realized he saw a vision.
Shortly, after Zechariah returned home, Elizabeth became pregnant
    And she hid herself from public view.
Elizabeth proclaimed, "Lord, You are gracious
    To take away the embarrassment of having no children."

The Story of Gabriel Promising Mary a Son

Mary was a pretty young woman, nearly always adorned with a smile. But today she wore a worried look as she walked toward the Nazareth Synagogue. Joseph was posting bands for their marriage.

"Suppose the elders say no?" Mary asked her mother. "They will approve," the mother assured her anxious daughter. Mary and her mother climbed the outside stairs to the synagogue loft where the women and children sat. They positioned themselves where they could see the elders when Joseph approached them.

"They must give approval to Joseph," Mary whispered to her mother.

Her mother only smiled. The people in the community knew that Mary was the most godly young woman in the synagogue. When Mary had caught Joseph's eye, all old grand mothers approved. They knew Joseph was a godly young man too.

18

Joseph rose and handed the parchment to the ruling elder. The elder nodded.

From the balcony, Mary watched without blinking. The elders, arranged in a row, were ready to make the announcement. Normally, the old men frowned when young men asked permission to marry. But for Joseph, their wrinkled, old eyes twinkled, their gray beards nodding up and down in approval.

After dinner, Mary rushed to the fig tree to pray. She loved to talk with God. It's the place where her father prayed.

O Lord God, may Your Kingdom come in our village…in our family…in my life….

Suddenly, she felt the presence of someone else under the tree; pivoting, she saw a stranger.

"Greetings," said the pleasant young man, smiling. "You who are highly favored, the Lord is with you."

Mary gasped. "Who are you?"

"Gabriel," the young man answered. "My name is Gabriel. Do not be afraid," he said. "You have found favor with God. You are to have a child. Your son shall be conceived in your womb, and when he is born, you shall give him the name Jesus."

Mary's heart leaped. In Hebrew, the language of her people, the name Jesus translated to Joshua, meaning "Jehovah saves." A little boy named Jesus would call to mind Joshua, the great leader who had defeated Israel's enemies.

Gabriel interrupted her thoughts. "God shall give your son the throne of his father, David. And His Kingdom shall never end."

The Deliverer? Mary thought. My son will be the Messiah? The coming of the Messiah had been foretold for hundreds of years. According to the prophecies, Mary was from the right family, descended from David. Her son could defeat the Romans just as the boy David had defeated Goliath, the Philistine giant. She said to the angel, "I am not yet married to

Joseph." The angel told Mary, "Joseph is not to be the father, the Holy Spirit shall come upon you and overshadow you, and the child shall be the Son of God."

Mary's thoughts tumbled one over another. How could she have a child without a father? What would people think? And what of Joseph?

As though he could read her thoughts, the angel reassured Mary. "Your cousin Elizabeth is too old to have children," he said. "She was said to be barren, but she has conceived. With God nothing is impossible."

Mary struggled briefly with her thoughts, but then she bowed her head. "Behold," she submitted, "I will be the Lord's handmaiden. Do to me what You have promised."

When she opened her eyes again, Gabriel was not there.

My Time to Pray

- Lord, may I be as submissive to Your plan for my life as Mary was to Your plan for her life.

- Please forgive me for any time in the past when I rebelled at Your plan for my life.

- May I be sensitive to Your plan when it comes to me.

Gabriel Promises Mary a Son

Luke 1:26-38

When Elizabeth was six months pregnant
        The angel Gabriel appeared to Mary
        A virgin who was engaged to Joseph;
        They were both in the family line of King David.

Gabriel greeted Mary, "Rejoice, Mary,
>   You are highly favored of God,
>   The Lord is with you."
Mary was confused with this greeting,
>   She didn't know what it meant.
Gabriel said, "Do not be afraid,
>   God has decided to use you
>   To be a blessing to all the world.
"You will conceive and deliver a Son,
>   You must call His name Jesus.
"He will have great influence on the world
>   And He will be the Son of the Most High God.
"God will give Your Son the throne of David
>   And He will rule over Israel forever."
Mary replied, "How can this happen,
>   I am a virgin,
>   And have not known a man?"
Gabriel answered, "The Holy Spirit will come on you,
>   Power from the Most High God will make it happen,
>   And you'll have a child who is the Son of God."
Gabriel continued, "Your Aunt Elizabeth
>   Has become pregnant with a child in her old age;
>   With God, nothing is impossible."
Mary answered. "I will be the Lord's handmaiden,
>   I am willing to be what the Lord wants me to be;
>   Let it happen, as you said."

Lord, I believe You can do miracles in my life,
>   *But my doubts are always lurking;*
>   *I believe, help Thou my unbelief.*

An Angel Speaks to Joseph

Matthew 1:1-25

Matthew wrote a biography of Jesus
    Emphasizing the Kingly ancestry of Jesus the Messiah.
Matthew included a family tree that showed Jesus
    Was the son of both King David and Abraham.
Matthew included the name of each generation,
    But the Holy Spirit had him include the
    Name of three women with questionable qualifications.
Matthew included Tamar, the daughter-in-law of *Judah*
    Whose disobedience and sin would have blocked
    The line leading to the Messiah.
But Tamar's faith and persistence
    Led to her son Perez that continued the Messianic line.
Matthew included Ruth, a Gentile, an outsider to the covenant,
    But her deep faith in You, led to her salvation;
She became the great grandmother of David when she
    Married into the line of the Messiah.
Matthew included Bathsheba, a married woman
    Who committed adultery with David.
But through the repentance of both she and David,
    Solomon was born who continued the line.

Lord, You included women of sin and unbelief
    In the line that led to Your Son, Jesus.
You did this because no one lives without sin,
    And You continually extend grace to each
    Just as You did to those three women.

Lord, when I don't believe You, or sin ignorantly,
    Please forgive me and extend Your grace to me.

Lord, the genealogy of Your son, Jesus, stretched
>For 14 generations from Abraham to David,
>For 14 generations from David to the Babylon Captivity,
>And 14 generations from the Babylonian Captivity to Jesus.

Joseph was engaged to Mary when it was discovered
>Mary was pregnant, but Joseph didn't know
>The pregnancy was by the Holy Spirit.
Because Joseph was a *man of high character*,
>He decided to privately break the engagement
>And not publicly embarrass Mary.
As he was praying and thinking about this matter,
>The angel of the Lord appeared and said to him,
>"Don't hesitate to take Mary as your wife.
"Her child has been conceived by the Holy Spirit,
>She will have a Son, name Him Jesus
>For He will save His people from their sin."

Lord, all this took place to fulfill the Scripture in Israel,
>"The virgin will conceive and give birth to a Son,
And He shall be called Immanuel,
>A name that means, 'God With Us.'"
Then Joseph did what the angel told him to do,
>He took Mary to his home;
But did not have sexual intercourse with her
>Until she gave birth to her Son, Jesus.

The Story of Mary Meeting Elizabeth

Mary walked up the rough-hewn path toward the village of Abia. She was 60 miles from home. Within her body was a human being, placed there by God.

"Maybe it is best if I stay with Elizabeth for a while," she had told her mother, concerned about what people in Nazareth would say.

Mary approached Elizabeth and Zechariah's house and stood for a moment in front of the open door. Then she walked into the room.

"Hello...I am Mary of Nazareth."

"Oh...oh...oh...!" Elizabeth cried out, reaching for her midsection. "My baby just leaped in my womb!"

Then all at once Elizabeth knew what was happening. She exclaimed loudly to her uninvited guest, "Blessed are you among women, and blessed is the fruit of your womb!"

At the sound of Mary's voice, the baby in Elizabeth's womb had leaped for joy. Somehow, her unborn baby had recognized the presence of the Messiah. "Why has the mother of our Lord come to see me?" Elizabeth asked.

But Mary couldn't give an earthly answer. She lifted her voice and praised God:

"My soul magnifies the Lord,
And my spirit has rejoiced in God my Savior.
For he has regarded the lowly state of his maidservant.
From this day forward, all generations will call me blessed."

Elizabeth and Mary talked until late in the evening. All that Elizabeth had learned about living with a man of God was absorbed by young Mary.

"What about Joseph?" Elizabeth asked. "What does Joseph think?"

Mary admitted that Joseph had at first sought to break their betrothal. But before he could gather the necessary witnesses, an angel of the Lord appeared to Joseph in a dream. He had instructed Joseph to take Mary as his wife and to call the baby Jesus.

My Time to Pray

- Lord, may I be as sensitive to Your presence coming into my life as Elizabeth and John the Baptist were when You entered the room.

- May I magnify You in all things as did Mary in her worship of You.

- May others see in me a trusting heart in You as Elizabeth saw that kind of trust in Mary.

Mary Visits Elizabeth

Luke 1:39-56

Mary left her home and went to Judah
 To visit Zechariah and Elizabeth.
She greeted Elizabeth as she entered the house,
 The babe leaped in Elizabeth's womb
 Because he knew he was in the presence of the Messiah.
Elizabeth was filled with the Holy Spirit
 And said, "Blessed are you among women
 And blessed is the child you bear.
"This is an honor that the mother of our lord should visit me;
 You believed the promises of our Lord
 That's why you've been given this great privilege."

Lord, help me always rejoice
 When I'm in the presence of Jesus,
 As did the babe, John the Baptist.

Mary's Song—The Magnificat

Mary responded to the Lord, "You are great, my God,
 My spirit rejoices in You, my Savior;
"You look upon this lowly servant,
 Now all generations will call me blessed.
"For You—the Mighty God—have done great things,

Holy is Your name.
"Your mercy extends to those who reverence You
    From one generation to another.
"You have done mighty works by Your arm,
    You have cast down the proud of heart.
"You have brought down mighty kings from their thrones,
    And you lift up the lowly.
"You have filled the hungry with good things,
    And sent the arrogant away empty.
"You have come to help Israel, Your people,
    And You have remembered to be merciful
    To Abraham and his descendants forever."

Mary stayed with Elizabeth three months,
    Then returned to her home.

Lord, may I ever praise You for using me,
    As Mary magnified You in song.

The Story of the Birth of John the Baptist

Zechariah sat with friends on the bench in front of his dwelling. He could hear the moans of Elizabeth from inside. Lord, make this delivery easy, was all he could think of to pray. Then Zechariah heard the wail of new life: "Waa-aa-aah…Waa-aah…Waa-aa-ah!" The neighbors heard the cry and came running.

"It's a boy!" the midwife announced as she emerged from the house. A cheer went up from the crowd gathering in Zechariah's yard.

Eight days later, the ceremony to circumcise the baby was held. The family tried to name the child after his father. An uncle announced, "Call the baby Zechariah."

"Yes! Zechariah," the relatives agreed. "Call the baby Zechariah."

Zechariah jumped to his feet and waved his arms in protest. "Ugh...ugh...ugh...."

He reached for the slate and chalk. The boisterous crowd grew silent. With shaking hand, Zechariah wrote in large bold letters: HIS NAME IS JOHN.

At the moment Zechariah finished writing, he felt something in his throat. He rubbed his neck with both hands, then tried to say something. He looked at the words he had written and read aloud, "His name is John."

My Time to Pray

- Lord, help me to have a trusting heart in all circumstance as Zechariah had living with the consequences of his unbelief.

- Lord, when I'm pressured by relatives and friends to do something contrary to Your will, may I be as firm in obeying You as was Zechariah.

The Birth of John the Baptist

Luke 1:57-66

Elizabeth gave birth to a son at the appointed time,
    The relatives and neighbors rejoiced with the parents.
When they came to circumcise him on the eighth day,
    The relatives tried to name him after his father.
Elizabeth protested saying, "Call him John,"
    The relatives said no one in the family had that name.
When they asked the father about the child's name,
    Zechariah asked for a tablet and wrote,

"His name is John."
Immediately, Zechariah was able to speak again,
>He praised You, and all the relatives joined him.
Everyone who heard about it wondered,
>"What will this child be?"
>For Your hand was with the child.

Lord, keep Your hand on me,
>*As You kept Your hand on John the Baptist.*

Zechariah's Song: The Benedictus

Luke 1:68-80

Zechariah was filled with the Holy Spirit
>And he spoke this prophecy,
"Blessed be You, Lord God of Israel,
>For You visited and rescued Your people.
"You have sent a mighty Deliverer
>To the people of Your servant, David,
>As You promised by the holy prophets.
"And the Deliverer will save us from our enemies,
>And from the hand of those who hate the Jews,
>So we can serve You all our days.
"And you my child, John, shall be called
>The prophet of the Most High God.
"John shall go before the Deliverer
>To prepare the way for His coming.
"John will tell the people about Your salvation
>And preach the forgiveness of sins,
"Showing us Your tender mercies that will
>Come to us like the rising of the sun.
"The Deliverer will give light to those living in darkness,
>And guide their feet in Your way."

And the child, John, grew strong physically and spiritually,
    And lived in the desert until
      His time to preach publicly to Israel.

Chapter 3

THE BIRTH OF JESUS

The Story of the Birth of Jesus in a Stable

"I could have made the trip without the donkey." The petite but very pregnant girl shut her eyes to the pain. "We can't afford this animal."

"The price is not important," replied her young husband. They had taken a shortcut from Jerusalem to Bethlehem and were trying to find a place to sleep before nightfall.

Bethlehem was the home of Mary's parents, and the Roman authorities had commanded everyone to return to his hometown to register for a census.

"Oh!" Mary clutched her midsection. "It's a labor pain." "Hold on," Joseph counseled. "Count the time between the pains."

Joseph was frantic as he banged at the wooden door of the inn. Mary pulled her cloak tighter against the wind. Her labor pains were closer together with every inn that turned them away. Bethlehem was swamped with pilgrims who had returned home for Rome's census.

"No room in this inn!" came a gruff voice from behind the door.

"We've got to have a place! My wife's having labor pains…a baby's coming!"

The innkeeper stepped out, closing the door behind him. Providentially, a pain hit and Mary moaned.

The innkeeper flinched. "There," he pointed to the stable. "You can deliver your baby in there."

"Thank you," was all Joseph could say as he led the donkey off.

He found some fresh hay for Mary to lie on, then he found some clean strips of white cloth. He prepared everything, then sat beside Mary to wait.

Two hours later, it happened—a healthy baby boy was born. Joseph didn't have to swat him. The baby's red face let out a bawl.

"Don't cry, Jesus," the new mother reached for her son. Baby Jesus nestled into Mary's loving arms.

My Time To Pray

- Lord, give me patience to accept Your regulations that make life difficult for me; and help me see Your plan for my life in them.

- Lord, help me joyfully accept the "closed doors" in my life. Lord, help me realize that when doors are closed to me, other opportunities will re-open to me.

The Birth of Jesus

Luke 2:1-7

Caesar Augustus commanded all people
>Had to return to their hometown to register
>For a census for tax purposes.
Then Joseph left Nazareth to return to Bethlehem
>Because he was in the royal line of David,
>His wife Mary was also in that line.
This happened when Quirinius

Became governor of Syria in 4 B.C.
Mary was pregnant and the birth imminent
　　So she gave birth while in Bethlehem.
The baby was born in a stable
　　Because there was no room in any of the inns.
Mary wrapped the baby in strips of cloths—swaddling clothes,
　　And laid Him in a feed trough.

The Story of Shepherds Watching Their Flocks

The breeze had died down and some of the shepherds came out of the small cave where they had taken shelter from the wind. Several others were already sleeping—waiting for their watch.

"Nothing happens this early in the evening," the younger shepherd moaned. His body was cold, his mind was cold, his world was cold.

"When nothing happens," the older shepherd said impatiently, "maybe we'll have peace." He had lost faith in God. The only thing he believed in was the tyranny of Rome because he had felt the sting of a Roman whip.

"When the Deliverer, the Son of David, comes, we'll have peace," said the younger man.

"Ha!" snorted the older shepherd. "Then I can go home, rather than hide up here in the hills." He paused, scratched his beard, and thought of a crime he committed when he was young. Hardened by years of running from the Roman authorities, he had finally taken work as a shepherd to hide.

The younger shepherd had prayed for the Messiah to come. The younger shepherd was hiding from the authorities for a different reason. He had sinned against his family and village, against God.

"When the Deliverer comes," the young man broke the silence, "He will purify my memory."

"What is that supposed to mean?" the older voice barked. "I've done something. I try to forget, but I can't."

A warm wind flushed the shepherds' faces. Then the night exploded in LIGHT!

Light from the heavens obliterated the darkness, blinding the two shepherds. With their hearts in their throats and their eyes stinging, they hid their faces.

"Do not be afraid," came a voice from the other side of the light.

"Wh-wh-what is it?" the young shepherd managed to ask.

"The voice is from Heaven. Only Heaven can be this bright," the older shepherd managed to say.

The younger shepherd shouted, "I see people in the sky!" The older man squinted toward the heavens. The glorious light appeared to be emanating from a breach in the sky. And flooding through the opening were angels. Thousands upon thousands of angels. And they were singing.

"Look…look…! There are so many I can't count them!" the youth cried.

"Do not be afraid," the voice behind the light repeated. "I have come to bring you tidings of great joy. Your Savior was born tonight in Bethlehem. He is Christ the Lord."

Then a magnificent sound flooded the night—a sound that flooded out the noise of past failures. The heavenly host praised God, singing: "Glory to God in the highest, And on earth peace, goodwill toward men!"

Then just as suddenly as the angels came, they were gone. "Let's go!" The younger shepherd leaped to his feet. "Where?" the other asked.

"Bethlehem! Didn't you hear? Our Savior was born in Bethlehem."

The shepherd in charge now spoke up. "We must bring the Savior a gift…a lamb."

"Mine," the young shepherd volunteered. "My lamb for the baby Savior."

Back in Bethlehem in the stable, Joseph bolted upright when he heard noises. Creeping to the door, he tried to be silent.

"Who is there?" Joseph spoke into the dark courtyard.

"We are shepherds," the lead shepherd replied. "Was a baby born here tonight?"

"Yes."

"We must see him. We have been told the child is the Savior sent from God."

Joseph opened the stable door wider. "Mary," he whispered. "Some shepherds want to see Jesus."

At Joseph's behest, the shepherds crowded through the door. But when the light shone upon the baby, the shepherds prostrated themselves in adoration.

Several minutes passed as the shepherds worshiped. Then one of them lifted his head and repeated the angels' song: "Glory to God in the highest, and on earth peace, goodwill toward men!"

One by one the shepherds looked up at the baby, Mary saw their eyes were streaked with tears.

The young shepherd whose secret sin had brought him to this place rose, the spotless lamb in his arms. He approached the feed trough where Jesus lay sleeping. Placing the lamb in the straw, he said simply, "For you. This lamb is in my place."

My Time To Pray

- Lord, may I worship You wholeheartedly like the shepherds. Lord, don't let any sin in my life keep me from worshiping You, as the sin of the older and younger shepherds stopped them.

- Lord, I will bring offerings with my worship, I will give You a tenth of all I have, and more importantly; I will give You myself.

Shepherds Visiting the Baby Jesus

Luke 2:8-20

The same evening the baby Jesus was born,
>   Shepherds were in an open field guarding their sheep.
Suddenly the sky lit up with an overwhelming light,
>   And a shining angel appeared to them;
>   The shepherds were scared out of their wits.
The angel announced to them, "Don't be frightened,
>   I have a wonderful message for you,
>   And for everyone else in the world.
"Tonight, the Deliverer—even the Lord—was born
>   In Bethlehem.
"You will recognize Him because He will be
>   Wrapped in swathes of cloths,
>   And will be lying in a feed trough."
Suddenly, the angel was joined by a gigantic choir
>   Praising God saying, "Glory to God
>   In the highest,
Peace to those who enjoy
>   God's good will."
When the angelic choir returned to Heaven,
>   The shepherds said to one another,
>   "Let's go see this baby God told us about."
When they ran to Bethlehem, they found
>   Mary, His mother, and the Babe lying in a manger.
Then the shepherds told everyone about the Babe,
>   And people were astonished at what they heard.

Lord, may I embrace the story of the Baby
>   *And worship Him with all my heart.*
May I tell everyone about the Baby
>   *And how Jesus came to forgive their sins.*

Dedication of the Baby Jesus

Luke 2:21-39

Jesus was circumcised eight days after He was born,
>   And they called His name Jesus,
>   Just as the angels instructed them.
Later, they returned to the temple
>   For the ritual cleansing of the mother
As was required by Moses in the Law,
>   "Every male that opened the womb
>   Shall be dedicated to the Lord.
"They did this with the offering of the poor,
>   Two young turtledoves and two pigeons."
There was an elderly man named Simon
>   Who looked for the restoration of the Kingdom.
Simeon lived blameless, and served God continually,
>   And he was filled with the Holy Spirit.
The Lord had revealed to Simeon he would
>   See the Deliverer before he died.
Simeon was led by the Spirit into the temple
>   On the day the Baby was to be dedicated.
Simeon took Jesus into his arms and blessed Him
>   Saying, "Lord, I have seen what You promised,
>   Now I am ready to die.
"For my eyes have seen Your salvation
>   Which all people will see one day.
"The Deliverer will be a light to the Gentiles,
>   And will bring glory to Your people, Israel."
Joseph and Mary marveled at Simeon's words,
>   Then Simeon said to Mary,
"This Child will be rejected by many in Israel
>   And God will judge their unbelief.
"But the Child will also be received by many in Israel,

And they shall be saved and rewarded of God."
There was also a prophetess named Anna
    Who was very old and had lived with her
    Husband only seven years after they were married.
She lived in the temple, worshiping God,
    Praying, and very often fasting.
She came along as Simeon finished his blessing;
    She gave thanks to God for the Child,
    Telling everyone the Deliverer had come.
Joseph and Mary then returned to their home,
    And the Child became physically strong
    And was filled with wisdom.

The Story of the Wise Men's Visit

"This house is wonderful," Mary chirped as she tidied the table. Mary and Joseph had settled down in Bethlehem when Jesus was born. Joseph had helped build several homes for the residents of Nazareth, but he had done some of his best work here in Bethlehem for his wife and son.

"This house will do for a while," he said, continuing his work. Mary and Joseph had chosen not to return to their hometown of Nazareth, because the rumors of a pregnancy out of wedlock made them uncomfortable.

They decided to remain in Bethlehem. "We'll be close to the temple for the baby," Joseph had reasoned. "If Jesus is to be the leader of our nation, he should live near the City of God."

Mary had opened the front and back doors to allow the cool morning air to ventilate the house. Joseph sat on a stool in the corner, carving.

"Look at the camels!" a small boy yelled outside their door.

Mary gathered Jesus in her arms, and she and Joseph stepped into the street, blinking against the sunlight. A block away a large crowd of villagers were gathered about a string of camels.

The lead camel driver was talking to Melki, the boy with the loud voice. The local youth lifted his arm and pointed toward Joseph. Now all eyes stared at Joseph and Mary—and the baby.

A man on a camel in a gold turban also pointed at Joseph and his family. He whispered to a servant, and the servant ran toward Joseph. Joseph spoke quietly to Mary. "Go in the house," he said. "There may be danger."

The servant bowed to Joseph. "We are searching for the one born king of the Jews."

How do they know? Joseph thought before answering. *What do they know?*

Sensing Joseph's apprehension, the servant again bowed deeply. Joseph recognized the curled toes on the man's sandals as a Persian fashion. The servant asked, "May we visit the young king this evening?"

Joseph again nodded, almost too shocked to speak.

That evening young Jesus sat under the meal table playing quietly. As the twilight faded, the toddler grew tired. Mary lit all the candles they had in the house and sat down for the first time that evening. Jesus crawled into her lap and dozed in her arms.

"THEY'RE COMING!" Joseph heard Melki yelling from down the street. Moments later there came a rapping at the door. Opening it, Joseph was greeted by the sight of a massive camel. The driver beat a stick on the camel's knee, and it knelt.

The servant who had spoken with Joseph earlier bowed. "Why did they ride?" Joseph asked. "It's a short distance from your camp.

"Royalty does not walk in dirty streets," the servant said.

With the tapestry robe held in one hand, the camel rider stepped onto the rug. He walked halfway to the house, then turning, snapped his fingers. Two servants lifted a heavy chest and followed him into the house. The second and third camels dislodged their distinguished riders in equally elegant fashion.

"We have come to worship the king of the Jews," the first and eldest of the noblemen spoke in flawless Greek.

The other two noblemen strained forward to see the child. Jesus let out a yawn, and they smiled when they saw it.

"We study the stars," the first nobleman explained. "The stars tell us God has sent a Savior." He said they were called magi, or wise men, because their lives were dedicated to studying the scrolls of the ancients.

"How did you know where to find us?" Joseph asked.

"We studied the holy books of the Jews. Your Scriptures promise a Deliverer, saying He will come from among the Jews."

"We believe this to be true," another of the magi spoke up.

"Your Scriptures tell of a star that will be a sign of his birth, so we began searching the sky for His star. About a year ago, a star that had not been in our sky just...appeared."

"His star," the third wise man insisted.

Jesus slept, blissfully unaware of the conversation in the room.

"His star began moving; we followed," the wise man's eyes flashed. "The star moved. We obeyed its direction. It led us to Jerusalem, we went immediately to see the one called Herod the Great to inquire of this child."

Joseph listened carefully as the wise men described Herod as a fat, arrogant, greedy man.

"I AM THE ONLY KING OF THE JEWS!" Herod had blustered, and demanded they tell him where the baby king could be found.

"We do not know," was their response. "We only followed the star."

"Go then," Herod had told the wise men. "Find him and bring me the location...I will come to worship the child."

Joseph's brow furrowed. Herod was ruthlessly cruel. An unsettling fear lodged in the mind of the young father.

The wise old leader clapped his hands for his valet. A cedar chest was placed on the floor before Mary and the child. Bending, the old man opened the chest. All present saw the light from the candle flames flicker off the gold coins inside it.

"Bless the Lord, O my soul," the wise man prayed in the Hebrew tongue.

Another of the magi then brought an expensive flask filled with myrrh, a rare, aromatic sap, and the third dignitary set a cask of frankincense before Mary. He opened the top and released the fragrance into the room.

After a time, the three magi arose. The oldest glanced to his traveling companions for approval, then he asked, "May we get a closer look...? We want to learn His features."

Mary unfolded the cloth from the child's face, then Jesus smiled at His guests.

My Time To Pray

- Lord, help me see that every gift that comes into my life is from You, then help me to use it properly in Your service.

- Lord, I know hard times will come sometimes in the future, help me see the ways You prepare me for them.

- When "marginal" people come into my life—like the magi—help me learn from them and accept the contributions they make to my life.

The Wise Men Visit The Child Jesus

Matthew 2:1-12

After Jesus was born in Bethlehem,
    Wise men—astrologists—came from the East,

41

Looking for the baby born King of the Jews.
They told King Herod that they saw His star in the East
    And followed it so they could worship the Baby.
King Herod was disturbed because the Roman Senate
    Had declared He was King of the Jews.
Herod assembled Jewish leaders to find out
    Where the prophets predicted the Deliverer would be born.
They quoted the Scripture, "You, Bethlehem in Judah,
    Are not the least important town
Because the Deliverer will come from You
    That will rule the people of Israel."
Herod met privately with the wise men
    To find out exactly when the star appeared.
Herod then sent the wise men to search for the Baby,
    And report back to him
    So he deceptively could also worship Him.
The wise men started toward Bethlehem and the Star
    Appeared again and led them,
    Stopping where the Child was.
Going into the house, they saw the Child with His mother
    And falling to their knees,
Then they gave Him their gifts: gold,
    Frankincense, and myrrh.
The wise men were warned in a dream
    Not to return to Herod,
    So they went home a different way.

Lord, I worship You as did the wise men,
    Whereas they gave You earthly wealth.
I also surrender all my earthly stuff to Your use
    But most importantly, I give You my heart.

The Story of Danger to the Baby Jesus

The town of Bethlehem dozed beneath a blanket of stars. Mary and Jesus slept peacefully. A dog barked in the distance, then let out a whimper. Joseph was awakened, but it was not the dog that had roused him. He had been startled out of sleep by a dream. In his dream,

He was working on a table, growing frustrated with his inability to balance the table's legs which he was building. So he set it aside and instead put the finishing touches on a cradle he had fashioned for the royal family. He stood back to admire his handiwork then he realized he had mistakenly made not a cradle, but a feed trough! Terror gripped his heart as a long shadow fell across the doorway. Had the king come for his cradle?

He turned to greet his highness, but it was not the king. There stood a beautiful angel, one with familiar features.

"Get up, Joseph," the angel-visitor warned. "An enemy is coming to kill the child."

Then Joseph knew. This was the angel-messenger who had foretold the birth of Jesus.

"Hurry," the angel warned. "Death comes after sun up. Go to Egypt. Take the child and his mother and stay until I tell you to return." Joseph nodded his willingness to obey.

There was a faint light in the east when Joseph led Mary out to the donkey. He helped her up, then brought her the bundled child. He threw two sacks filled with gold, frankincense, and myrrh over the animal that was their "money" to pay for the trip. By the time they made their way out of Bethlehem, the light was beginning to reveal the road ahead.

A few miles out of Bethlehem the donkey refused to go any farther. The donkey jerked his head angrily against Joseph's direction. The donkey pulled Joseph toward a little stream at the side of the road.

"What's wrong?" Mary was concerned.

"We left so quickly. I didn't give him water."

Mary decided it was a good time to feed Jesus and found a secluded spot out of the breeze. Joseph led the animal into the stream to drink.

Moments later, Joseph heard shouts coming from the direction of Jerusalem. Then Joseph heard the unmistakable tramp of Roman soldiers.

"Stay hidden in the rocks," Joseph instructed his wife.

The troops were led by a centurion dressed in battle gear. Spotting the stream, the centurion stopped to give his horse a drink. The horse waded into the shallow water near the rocks where mother and child were hidden.

Mary prayed, *Lord, don't let Jesus cry.* The toddler closed His eyes and slept.

In the darkness, the Roman officer couldn't see into the bushes, but Joseph could see out of the bushes. He saw the centurion clearly enough. He wanted to run, but held his ground. The donkey stood silently.

The centurion jerked at his reins and the white horse ascended the bank from the stream and took up its trot beside the soldiers. With hands on their swords and death on their minds, they marched toward Bethlehem.

Quickly Joseph and Mary were back on the road. By midmorning, they had traveled far enough that their fears subsided.

Two nights later they were halfway to Egypt, and stopped for the night at an oasis. They were almost ready to go to sleep when a loud gruff voice was heard approaching.

The burly new arrival dropped his pack. Sticking his feet into the cool water, he complained of walking all day to anyone who would listen.

"I never want to see another Jew!" the voice carried over the water. "Yesterday, King Herod killed all the baby boys in Bethlehem!" The traveler went on to describe how the Roman soldiers had stacked the bodies of the babies near the well. Herod had ordered the death of all male children two years old and younger because of a rumor that a rival to his throne had been born in Bethlehem.

Mary looked at Joseph through the evening shadows. She silently wondered, *Why was our Jesus saved?*

My Time To Pray

- Lord, help me joyfully give up friends and home when it comes time for You to lead me to a new home and place to live.

- Lord, protect me from unseen dangers that I am not aware of and protect me from dangers I know.

- Lord, when I come face-to-face with danger, give me poise, courage, and show me how to react.

- Lord, I don't understand why anyone would kill another; I pray for murderers that they would repent and turn to You for forgiveness.

Slaughter of Babies in Bethlehem

Matthew 2:13-18

After the wise men left Mary and the Child,
> The angel of the Lord spoke to Joseph in a dream,
"Get the child and His mother and escape to Egypt,
> King Herod will try to kill Him;
> Stay there until I tell you to come back."

Joseph immediately took the child and His mother
    And left for Egypt.
Then the prophecy of the Lord was fulfilled,
    "I will call my Son out of Egypt."
When Herod realized the wise men deceived him,
    He sent soldiers to Bethlehem to kill every child
    Who was two years or younger.
Then, the prophecy of Jeremiah was fulfilled,
    "Screams and mourning were heard in Ramah,
    Rachael was sobbing for her children
    And she would not be comforted
    Because they no longer lived."

Chapter 4

EGYPT AND BEYOND

The Story of Baby Jesus in Egypt

Mary and Joseph had settled in a small Egyptian town. Joseph worked in a carpenter shop, making furniture for Egyptian customers.

One night a sudden gust of wind blew through the room and Joseph awoke in the darkness. A rooster had crowed, but dawn was not near. He prayed, *Lord, what are you trying to say to me?*

Joseph listened, but nothing came to him and he soon drifted off to sleep.

He was back in his shop in Bethlehem, working on the table...again. Two years, and he had been unable to balance the legs. Then Jesus his young son entered the shop. Little Jesus walked over to the table and, taking a saw in his small hand, shortened the errant leg. He stepped away and looked at his father for approval.

Joseph nudged the table, but it no longer wobbled. He turned to Jesus. "How did you do this, my son?"

Jesus smiled again and said, "I must be about my father's business." Joseph then looked past Jesus toward the door. There, towering above the doorway once again was the angel-messenger of God.

The angel-visitor spoke. "Take Jesus and his mother and return to the land of Israel. Herod is dead."

During the next few days, Joseph wrapped up his business. On the appointed day, the family left Egypt, never to return. Three days later they stopped at the same oasis where they had spent the night on their flight from Bethlehem. That night Joseph lay on his pallet. He soon slipped into sleep and dreamed.

The angel once again visited, *"Do not go to Jerusalem," the angel said to Joseph. "There is danger waiting there for Jesus. Return to Nazareth in Galilee."*

Joseph thought about Galilee. They had fled Nazareth because of the rumors. He was afraid they would criticize Mary. Then Joseph realized that only embarrassment faced them in Nazareth.

In Jerusalem, his son faced death. "It will be as you say," he told the messenger. "I will return to Nazareth."

My Time To Pray

- When I'm put in strange or uncomfortable situations, help me to adapt; then help me to do my business, and keep me faithful to You when I'm separated from family and friends.

- Lord, I believe there are guardian angels; I accept their protection and I thank You for them.

- May I surrender to You in all circumstances, as did Mary and Joseph.

Jesus' Exile in Egypt

Matthew 2:19-23

The Lord sent an angel to Joseph after Herod died,

    Telling him to return to the land of Israel,

    "Those who tried to kill Jesus are now dead."

So Joseph took the child and Mary and headed

    Toward the land of Israel.

Then Joseph heard that Archelaus was now king

    So he was afraid to go to Bethlehem.

So, the Lord spoke to Joseph in a dream telling him

    To go back to Galilee and his home in Nazareth.

Then the prophecy was fulfilled,

    "He (Jesus) shall be called a Nazarene."

The Story of Jesus Leaving Egypt for Nazareth

Mary and Joseph had lived in Egypt for three years. Now they were back in Nazareth. Near the back of the house, Joseph had built a carpenter shop. Mary was pregnant with their third child. She called her son into the house. "Jesus, it is time to learn how to write." Mary handed him a stylus. "Hold this pen between your fingers like this."

Within a year, he was copying his favorite psalms. "Jesus, if you're going to be a king," Mary said to him, "then you must write a complete copy of the Scriptures, just like a king. Then the thoughts of Scripture will belong to you."

So each day Jesus copied a different psalm and memorized it, repeating it flawlessly to his mother.

My Time To Pray

- Lord, help me see Your guiding hand in my life and help me follow You today.

- Lord, help me learn the Scriptures as did the young Jesus.

- Lord, I will read and study Your Word each day.

Chapter 5

THE GOSPEL OF JOHN

John 1:1-18

The first three Gospels—Matthew, Mark, and Luke—tell the human side of the birth of Jesus because Jesus was totally human. The Gospel of John tells the divine side of Jesus coming into the world because Jesus was totally God.

Lord, I worship Jesus Who is from the beginning;
    Jesus is the Word Who tells me
    All that You are.
Jesus, the Word, was face to face with You throughout eternity
    Because Jesus is God.

Lord, I worship Jesus, the mighty God Who created all things,
    And without Him was nothing created;
    Jesus does all the things that You do.

Lord, I worship Jesus who has all life in Himself
    And gives life to all His creation.
Jesus is the life of God who is the
    Light to all lost in a dark hideous world.
Jesus shines in the hostile darkness,
    But the darkness doesn't even know He exists.

Lord, John the Baptist was a prophet sent by You
    Who came to tell all about the shining Light,
    That through the Light, all might be saved.
John the Baptist was not the saving light
    But was the human sent to point everyone to the Light.

Jesus is the true saving Light
      Who offers spiritual light to all in the world.

Lord, Jesus came to the world that He created,
      But those living in the world
      Did not recognize Jesus as their Creator.
Jesus came to His own people—the Jews—
      And they refused to recognize Him.
But as many as recognize Jesus and receive Him,
      He will make them Your children,
      Simply because they believe in the authority of Jesus' name.
They will be born again by Your power,
      Which is not being born of blood,
      Or the choice of people, or of flesh.

Lord, I worship Jesus, the Word, who became flesh,
      And lived as man among men.
Jesus had all the celestial glory of Heaven
      But He clothed His heavenly glory with human flesh;
      God living in flesh was the greatest glory of all.
Jesus is Your uniquely begotten Son,
      And has all Your grace and truth.

Lord, John the Baptist said of Jesus, "This is the Messiah
      Whom I introduced to the world;
      Jesus comes after me, but is pre-eminently before me."

Lord, I received the full benefits of Jesus;
      His grace was offered and my need of grace was fulfilled.
The law of Moses condemned me to death,
      But grace and truth by Jesus gave me life.
I could never have seen You, the eternal Father,
      But Jesus Christ came from Your bosom
      To show us what You, our Father is like.

The Story of 12-year-old Jesus in the Temple

The Bar Mitzvah of Jesus

"Look, Mary!" Joseph called to his wife. "I always get a thrill when I first see the Eternal City set high on Mount Zion."

Mary and Joseph had left home three days earlier from Nazareth with a caravan of family and friends. The annual pilgrimage to Jerusalem for the Passover was a festive occasion.

Joseph and Mary were taking their 12-year-old son, Jesus, for his first visit to the temple. Jesus was now of an age to observe the requirements of Jewish law, and the Law required that Jewish men attend the feasts of Passover, Pentecost, and Tabernacles in Jerusalem.

Jesus scooted up the path ahead of his parents toward Jerusalem. He seemed pulled to the city.

The next day, they hastened through the crowded corridors of the city, the family entered the temple. The clamor of the streets died away and the sweet peace of the psalms rippled through the courtyard of the temple. Suddenly Jesus dropped to his knees beside Joseph. This experience had been a long time coming, and Jesus wanted to drink deeply from it.

Without coaxing, his childlike voice blended with the resonant sounds of mature priests as they repeated, "Hear, O Israel: The Lord our God is one Lord! You shall love the Lord with all your heart, with all your soul and strength."

The family had left Jerusalem at noon for the return home to Nazareth. Walking half a day, they reached El Birech, an oasis north of Jerusalem.

"We'll set up camp over there," Joseph pointed to a grassy place. He nodded to his son James. "Find your brother Jesus and gather some sticks for a fire."

When James returned he said, "I can't find Jesus."

Mary's heart jumped. "Run up ahead and check the campsites," Joseph commanded James. "Ask if they have seen Jesus."

Joseph left the oasis and began retracing their route back toward Jerusalem, asking anyone he met along the way about Jesus. James returned and reported that no one had seen Jesus all day. Evening was darkening when Joseph returned to camp. He had not found his son. "Pack up everything," he barked to the younger children, "Jesus must still be in Jerusalem." Within minutes, the family was back on the road.

By the next day, the parents were frantic. Joseph and Mary knew that Jesus could take care of himself in Nazareth, but this was a metropolitan city. They were at their wits' end.

Then Joseph remembered the strange look on his son's face when they worshiped at the temple. "Let's look in the temple," Joseph said. They hurried to the temple. Joseph managed to ask the first priest he saw, "Have you seen a young boy here? Beautiful olive skin? A child's white tunic, well-washed but worn?"

"All the children here look like that," the kindly priest laughed. "But there is a child sitting with the teachers of the Law; he's causing quite a commotion...."

Joseph and Mary didn't wait for him to elaborate. Dashing into a courtyard, they saw a tightly grouped crowd of people. There at the center was Jesus, standing in the midst of several bearded teachers and scholars.

"Let me put this question to you...." Jesus directed a question to the scholars. They were sitting at his feet!

Mary could not contain herself any longer. With a voice of concern mixed with relief, she called out, "Son! Why have you worried us?"

The crowd was silent. No one dared speak.

"We have searched all of Jerusalem for you..." Mary said. Twelve-year-old Jesus sensed anguish in his mother's voice. "Why didn't you look first in my Father's house?" he asked.

"Didn't you know that I would be about my Father's business?"

My Time To Pray

- Lord, give me a deeper desire to attend Your house and to join others to worship You there.

- Teach me the value of Your presence in my life. Help me to be diligent to get children into Your house to learn of You and worship You.

Twelve-year-old Jesus in Jerusalem

Luke 2:41-52

Jesus went with His parents to Jerusalem for
>The annual Passover Feast
>For He was 12 years old.
As the parents left Jerusalem for home,
>Jesus stayed in Jerusalem
>But His parents didn't know it.
After a day's journey, they went looking for Him,
>Thinking Jesus was with relatives.
When they failed to find Jesus, they returned to Jerusalem
>To search for Him.
After three days, they found Jesus sitting among the teachers,
>Listening to them and asking questions.
All who heard Jesus were greatly impressed
>At His level of comprehension
>And the difficult questions He asked them.
Joseph and Mary were astonished when they saw Him,
>And Mary asked Him,
"Son, why have You treated us like this?
>Your Father and I have been worried to death."
Jesus answered, "Why were you searching for Me?

Didn't you know that I had to
    Be about My heavenly Father's business?"
Jesus returned to Nazareth with them and
    Was under authority to them.
His mother didn't forget any of these incidents
    And meditated on them often.
Jesus grew in mental ability and physical strength
    And was respected by God and men.

Lord, I love the boy Jesus as much as
    I love the Savior on the Cross;
    Help me to always follow Him.

John the Baptist Begins Preaching

Matthew 3:1-12

In the 15th year of Emperor Caesar Tiberius,
    Herod was the Tetrarch of Galilee and Pontius Pilate
    Was governor of Judaea.
Philip ruled Ituranea and Lysanias ruled Abilene
    And the High Priest was Caiaphas.
The Word of God came to John the Baptist
    And he went through all Judaea
    Preaching baptism of repentance for the forgiveness of sins.
John quoted the Book of Isaiah proclaiming
    "I am the voice of one crying in the wilderness,
    Make ready the way for the Lord,
    Make straight paths for Him,
    Fill in every valley
    And make level the hills and mountains,
    Take the curves out of crooked roads,
    Smooth out rough streets,
    So all mankind can receive God's Savior."

John preached to the crowds,

> "Who warned you to escape the coming wrath?
> Show good fruit if you have repented;
> Do not think you can escape judgment
> Just because you are Abraham's children.
> God can make children of Abraham
> From these stones in the desert.
> "Every tree that doesn't grow good fruit
> Will be cut down and thrown into the fire;
> The axe is ready to cut down your tree."

The crowd cried out, "What must we do?"

> John answered their questions:
> "If you have two coats, give one to the poor,
> If you have extra food, give it to the hungry."

Corrupt tax collectors asked John, "What must we do?"

> John replied, "Don't threaten or brutalize people,
> Be satisfied with your pay."

Everyone anticipated their Deliverer would soon appear,

> And many thought John was the Messiah.

John answered them, "I only baptize with water,

> The One following me will baptize with fire
> And with the Holy Spirit;
> I am not worthy to unloose his sandal straps.

"The One following me will separate real believers

> Who represent good grain
> From chaff that represent false believers.

"He will store the good grain in His barns,

> But will burn the chaff in eternal fire."

Lord, John preached the truth and I believe it,
> *I believe in Jesus the Messiah of Israel;*
> *He will protect me in the Day of Judgment.*

The Story of the Jews Questioning John the Baptist

Jesus walked through the bushes toward the Jordan River near Bethabara, a small village north of the Dead Sea. The sound of water told him the river was close.

Then he heard a voice preaching to a crowd. As Jesus stepped out of the underbrush, the piercing bass voice of John the Baptist rang out, "REPENT! Prepare the way of the Lord."

Jesus smiled when he saw John the Baptist. John stood in water ankle-deep in water as he spoke, wild and uncivilized in his appearance. Around him people sat on the rocks on the bank. All kinds of people had come to hear John—slaves, Roman soldiers, mothers with children.

Then Jesus noticed a cluster of men who were not enjoying the sermon. These were religious leaders, scribes and Pharisees. One of them interrupted John to ask: "Who are you?"

"I am the voice of one crying in the wilderness," John answered.

"Are you the Deliverer?" another demanded.

"No! I am here to prepare the way for Messiah." John had lived apart from the villages for many years. He subsisted on a diet of locusts and honey and had little use for the religious establishment.

"Then why are you baptizing?" one of them asked him. John was usurping the authority of the temple. He baptized people rather than sending them to the temple to offer sacrifices. Only Gentiles who wished to become Jews were required to undergo such ritual cleansing. By baptizing Jews, John made no distinction between Gentiles and God's chosen people.

One of the scribes spoke up angrily, saying, "Are we also to be baptized?"

"You brood of vipers!" John shouted, incensed. "The axe is already at the root of the trees, and every tree that does not produce good fruit will be cut down and thrown into the fire."

"What should we do then?" someone in the crowd called out.

"The man with two tunics should share with him who has none, and the one who has food should do the same."

A Roman soldier sitting with a few comrades stood up. "And what should we do?"

John replied, "Don't extort money and don't accuse the people falsely."

The people murmured, again wondering if John might be Christ, their Deliverer. John answered, saying, "I baptize you with water. But One more powerful than I will come, whose sandals I am not fit to carry. Even now He is among us."

Scandalized, the scribes and Pharisees refused to hear any more. They scooped up fistfuls of sand and threw it into the air, cursing John. Then they departed.

The following day, John again preached to the hundreds assembled at the river. When he gave his invitation to the people to be baptized, Jesus stepped into the river.

Jesus was unremarkable in appearance, his features plain. But when John saw Jesus coming to him, the Baptist stopped in mid-sentence. With the confidence of Heaven and assurance in his heart, John pointed to Jesus: "BEHOLD, THE LAMB OF GOD WHO TAKES AWAY THE SIN OF THE WORLD!"

A murmur started low but grew steadily. "Does John know this man?" "What does the Baptist mean, 'Lamb of God'?" "Surely John doesn't believe this man is the Messiah!"

Jesus splashed through the shallow water to where John was standing. Each man looked into the other's soul. Finally, Jesus broke the silence. "I am ready to be baptized," he said, smiling.

"You are the One sent by God," John said. "I need to be baptized by You."

"Allow this," Jesus said, "because it is the right and proper thing to fulfill all that God requires."

So, John the Baptist placed his hands on the chest and back of Jesus and dipped Him into the waters. When he raised Him from the river, Jesus was smiling. The crowd on the riverbank did not understand what they had just seen.

Then it happened. Silently...harmlessly...just as a dove rests on the branch of a tree, the Holy Spirit descended from Heaven and rested gently on Jesus.

Jesus stood praying there in the shallow waters when a sound came like thunder. It was a voice from Heaven. Everyone heard it, though many were unsure of what they heard. Still, those who truly believed, whose hearts swelled at this remarkable visitation, heard clearly the voice of the living God. "YOU ARE MY BELOVED SON, IN WHOM I AM WELL PLEASED."

My Time To Pray

- Lord, may I be willing to be baptized in water as was Jesus. Lord, I know when I'm dipped in water, I'm identifying with Jesus' death and burial. When I'm raised from the water, I'm identified with Jesus' resurrection. May I live by the power of the new life I get from His resurrection. I believe in the Trinity: Jesus the Son of God was baptized, the Father spoke from Heaven and the Holy Spirit descended on Jesus as a dove.

- Lord, I'm pleased with all that Jesus was and did just as the Father was pleased with Him.

Religious Leaders Question John the Baptist

John 1:9-28

The religious establishment sent delegates
    To interrogate John the Baptist, asking,
    "Who are you?"
John told them he was not the Messiah;
    Then they asked, "Are you Elijah
    Or the prophet who will come at the end of the age?"
John said, "No, I am the voice of one crying in the wilderness,
    Repent and prepare for Messiah."

Lord, may I be a clear witness to Jesus,
    Pointing all to Christ, as did John the Baptist.

The religious delegates asked why John was baptizing.
    He answered, "I baptize with water,
    But there is one among us who will baptize
    With the Spirit of God."

Lord, I want to be immersed into the Holy Spirit
    As John the Baptist promised would happen.

Part Two

Jesus—The Son of God and Man

Chapter 6

JESUS, DISCIPLES, AND MIRACLES

The Story of Jesus' First Disciples

The young fishermen had grown up together in Bethsaida. Andrew and John trusted each other. As followers of John the Baptist, they had often talked late into the night about the promised Messiah. "Get ready for His coming," the Baptist preached.

Yesterday, Andrew and John had witnessed the baptism of a man named Jesus, whom John the Baptist had declared was the "Lamb of God." Both friends had heard the voice of God from Heaven saying, "THIS IS MY BELOVED SON...."

When they saw Jesus walking among the crowds the next day, Andrew and John followed Him, at first from a distance. After a few moments, Jesus stopped and confronted them. "What do you seek?"

Andrew, spoke up. "Rabbi ..." he spoke the title "rabbi" with reverence, surprising his friend John with his use of the honorific word for "teacher." "Rabbi, where are You living?"

"Come and see." Jesus said, "We'll eat together."

Soon it would be dark, Jesus, Andrew, and John settled around a simple meal.

"If you are the Messiah," Andrew asked, "why did you not preach to the multitudes today?" Andrew believed the Jews would acknowledge their Deliverer and follow Him. John pointed out that more than a thousand men had been present that day at the river; they could have formed the nucleus of a formidable army.

"My Kingdom will not come by war," Jesus explained. "I must rule the hearts of people. I must rule within before I rule without."

Jesus taught them what the Messiah would do, tracing God's plan for the redemption of mankind. Beginning with the Torah—the first five books of Scripture—through the books of the prophets Jesus showed them what God had said about the coming Anointed One. And Jesus had piercing questions for these young men.

"What does God want you to do with your life?"

Neither man was sure how to answer.

"When will you begin searching for God's will?"

"Now," they promised.

"Come, follow Me." Jesus said. "Then go tell others about the Kingdom."

The next morning the young men were gone. But Jesus knew they had not rejected what He taught them; these were true seekers whose hearts were open to the things of God.

Later, as Jesus was returning on the road to Galilee, Andrew came walking swiftly from the opposite direction. Someone was with him. Andrew waved, then yelled, "This is my brother Simon. I told him you are the Messiah."

A tall man with a broad chest, and a red beard, Simon was ten years older than Andrew. "Are you the Christ?" he yelled as they approached.

Jesus laughed at the boldness of the man, then looked into his eyes, "You are Simon, son of Jonah," Jesus said to him, "but from now on you shall be called Peter. You will be like a rock."

"You are a blunt speaker," Jesus continued, "I will need you to help build my Kingdom."

Turning to Andrew, Jesus said, "I will need your sensitivity and insight in the Kingdom. You are careful of people's feelings."

They walked on. Soon they met young John and his brother James. Brawny and tall, James didn't say much, though like his brother he had a fiery temperament.

"I don't like to speak," James said to Jesus, "but if You are who they say, I'll do anything You ask."

My Time To Pray

- Lord, may I follow You as did Andrew and John. Lord, help me to reach my relatives to become devoted followers of Jesus, as Andrew and John got their brothers to follow You.

- Lord, give me sensitive eyes so I can see people in the daily crowd around me who want to be Your followers.

- Lord, my talents are different than others. Use my unique gifts in Your service; just as You used the four fishermen, although each was different from the other.

Jesus Meets Six Disciples

John 1:28-51

John the Baptist said, "I saw the Spirit descend on the Messiah when He was baptized with water."

The next day John the Baptist told two of His disciples,
"Behold the Lamb of God."
As Andrew and John were following Jesus, He asked,
"What do you want?"
That evening Andrew and John talked at length to Jesus;

The next day Andrew told his brother Simon,
"We have found the Messiah,"
And Andrew brought his brother to Jesus.

Lord, may I be zealous to tell family and friends about Jesus
And may I bring them to know Jesus.

Jesus changed Simon's name to Peter
Which meant he was firm and solid as a stone.

Lord, may I be strong and courageous in my life.

The next day when Jesus saw Philip, He said, "Follow Me";
Philip was from the same hometown as Andrew and Peter.
Philip told his friend Nathaniel,
"We have found the Messiah."

Lord, may I find answers to all my questions in Jesus.

Nathaniel was skeptical, "Can any good thing come out of
Nazareth?" Philip just said, "Come and see."

Lord, help me always focus my sight on Jesus and see the
greatness of His character.

When Jesus saw Nathaniel He said,
"You are a sincere Israelite, you are an honest seeker."
Nathaniel asked, "How do you know me?"
Jesus revealed His divine omnipresence by saying, "I
saw You talking under the fig tree to Philip when he told
you About Me."

Nathaniel responded, "Jesus, You are the Son of God,
You are the King of Israel."

Lord, may I worship You when I learn of Your divine Sonship;
I yield myself to Your kingly rule.

Nathaniel believed in Jesus because of what Philip told him;
>But Jesus said, "You'll see much greater things than this.
"You'll see Heaven opened and the angels of God going up and
>Down upon Me, the Son of Man."

Lord, I believe what I learn of Jesus in Scripture,
>*I want to see greater things in my experience;*
>*May Christ be magnified in my life.*

The Story of the First Miracle—Water to Wine

"JESUS!" the feminine voice rang out. The young Galilean men gathered around Jesus turned to see a middle-aged woman waving to them.

"Jesus," she repeated the name of her oldest son. "Thank You for coming to Your cousin's wedding," Mary said.

They were interrupted by a demanding voice from the house. "Mary, the wine is running low!" Levi, the master of ceremonies, was an elderly man, short and thin. His voice was quiet, but insistent.

"JESUS!" Levi raised his voice when he recognized his nephew. Jesus introduced His disciples to His uncle, who in turn responded, "You must come and eat with us."

After meeting the guests and the families of the wedded couple, the young men took their places at the table.

"Bring them a plate of food," Mary instructed the servants. Quickly, warm bread appeared, and lamb stew.

At the head of the table, Levi told stories. There was laughter and there were more than a few red faces.

While Levi was speaking, Mary whispered to Jesus, "There's no more wine. The pitchers are empty. What am I to do?"

"Why do you come to Me? You are responsible for the food at this wedding," Jesus said to her.

"But I am not the one who will bear the shame," Mary thought aloud. "Levi and this poor young couple will suffer the humiliation of failing to provide for their guests."

Jesus left the festivities and walked outside to the back of the house. The servants followed, watching Him.

Against a corner of the house were six water pots, each of a different size and color. Jesus turned to the servants and said, "Fill each one to the top with water. Then take the wine to Levi."

The servants quickly took small vessels and filled the larger pots. Then, picking up the pots, they started toward the door.

"Attention, everyone!" Levi managed to conceal his relief at the arrival of additional wine. "Let's have a toast to the bride and groom."

The table grew silent. Panic flashed in the servants' faces. They placed a large pot on the floor on either side of Levi. Levi took his cup and dipped into the water pot. Since it was customary for the master to drink first, he put the cup to his lips.

"Ah-h-h," he sighed. Then Levi's crinkled eyes and deep smile suddenly vanished. He stared unbelievingly into his cup. "Why have you hidden the best wine until now? Every man sets out the good wine first. But you have saved the best for last!"

Levi laughed. The groom laughed. The guests all laughed. But the servants began jabbering among themselves. John turned to his brother James and whispered, "The servants claim Jesus turned water into wine."

The disciples talked excitedly between themselves. Was this possible?

"Tell us what you are saying!" Levi called loudly to James and John.

John spoke carefully. "The vintage you are drinking came from the pots that catch rain. An hour ago, it was not wine, but water."

Levi commanded that the servants be brought to him. "Where did you get this wine?" he demanded.

The head servant spoke with his eyes downcast. "Your nephew, the son of Mary, commanded us to fill the pots to the brim with water. We do not know how He did it, but the water became wine!"

The room fell silent. All eyes turned to Jesus, but Jesus was not there. He had departed before the wine was served.

My Time To Pray

- Lord, You have many ways to supply my needs, thank You for them all.

- Lord, thank You for going beyond supplying my basic necessities; thank You for supplying wine that is better than that which was served at first.

- Lord, I'm glad You recognized the institution of marriage by attending a wedding and blessing it with Your provision.

- Lord, help me reverence my parents—or their memory—as Jesus who had a proper relationship to His mother.

- Lord, help me see and act on the importance family has in my life.

- Lord, I believe in the miraculous, help me accept it when You send it into my life.

Jesus' First Miracle

John 2:1-11

On the seventh day after His baptism,
> Jesus was in Cana where a marriage ceremony was held;
> His mother was also there.

Jesus and His six disciples were invited to the meal
>   When the wine ran out; the mother of Jesus
>   Said to Him, "There is no more wine."
Jesus answered, "Why do you turn to me for help?
>   It is not the time to reveal who I am."
Jesus' mother told the servants,
>   "Do whatever He tells you."
There were six stone water pots available to them,
>   Each one held 20 to 30 gallons.
Jesus said to the servants, "Fill them to the brim with water."
>   Then He said, "Take them to the master of ceremonies."
The servants carried the water to the one in charge;
>   When they arrived the water had turned to wine,
>   Then the master of ceremonies toasted the wine.
He called the bridegroom to ask, "Why have you
>   Kept back the best wine until now?
"People usually serve their best wine first?
>   When the guests have drunk a lot
>   Then a poorer quality is served."
The servants who carried the water pots
>   Knew what happened.
This was the first miracle that Jesus did
>   And His disciples believed in Him.

Lord, I believe in You for who You are,
>   *Not for the things You do for me.*

The Temptation of Jesus

Matthew 4:1-11; Mark 1:12; Luke 4:1-13

Jesus was led by the Holy Spirit into the wilderness
>   To be tempted by satan.
Jesus fasted for 40 days and He was hungry,

Then in His hour of physical weakness
The tempter came tempting Him, saying,
"If You are the Son of God,
Turn these stones into bread."
But Jesus answered the tempter by quoting Scripture,
"Man shall not live by bread alone,
But by every Word that comes out of the mouth of God."
Next, the tempter took Jesus into Jerusalem
And they stood on its highest pinnacle.
The temper said, "If You are the Son of God,
Throw Yourself down." Then the tempter
Quoted Scriptures to entice Jesus,
"God will put You in charge of His holy angels;
They will catch You in their hands
So You will not be smashed on the stones."
Jesus answered the tempter by quoting Scripture,
"Do not put the Lord your God to a test."
Next, the tempter took Jesus to a high mountain
And showed Him the kingdoms of the world.
The tempter said, "I will give You all of these
If You will prostrate Yourself to worship me."
Then Jesus answered, "Get away from Me."
Jesus quoted Scripture, "You must worship
The Lord Your God, and serve Him only."
Then the tempter left Jesus alone
And angels came to meet His needs.

Lord Jesus, I praise You for overcoming temptation
So You remained the perfect Lamb of God
To die for my sins.
Help me overcome temptation when I'm tempted,
So I can be victorious for You.

So Jesus began preaching everywhere, "Repent,
> For the kingdom of Heaven is at hand."
Thus Jesus fulfilled the prophecy about His ministry:

> *Land of Zebulum and Naphtali,*
> *The way to the sea from the far side of Jordan,*
> *Called Galilee of the nations,*
> *The people that live in darkness*
> *Will see a great light.*
> *Those who live in the land of His shadow of death*
> *Will be illuminated by the Light.*

Jesus Calls Fishermen

Matthew 4:18-21; Mark 1:16-20

Then Jesus returned to Capernaum after the temptation;
> As He walked by the Sea of Galilee He saw
> Peter and Andrew casting their nets into the sea.
Jesus called out to them, "Come, be my disciples,
> I'll teach you how to catch people";
> Immediately they left their nets and followed Jesus.
A little farther, Jesus saw two more fishermen, James and John;
> They were mending their nets
> With their father Zebedee and the servants.
Jesus called them also to be His disciples;
> Immediately they left their nets
> To follow Jesus.

Lord, teach me instant obedience
> *So I can serve You better.*

Jesus Attends Sabbath Services

Mark 1:21-28

It was the Sabbath so Jesus went into the synagogue
>   As was His custom every Saturday.
Because Jesus was a visiting rabbi, the elders
>   Gave Him an opportunity to teach the people.
They were amazed at what Jesus said
>   And the way He said it;
>   Jesus' words were authoritative, not like the others.
There was a demon-possessed man in the congregation,
>   He screamed out to Jesus.
"Jesus of Nazareth, what do you want with me?
>   Have you come to destroy me?"
>   This was the demon speaking through the man.
The demon said to Jesus, "I know who you are,
>   You are the Holy One of God;
>   You are El Elyon, the possessor of Heaven and earth."
Jesus commanded the demon, "Be quiet!"
>   Then Jesus said, "Come out of the man."
The demon screamed loudly,
>   Then the man shook uncontrollably
>   With convulsions,
>   And the demon came out of the man.
The crowd was amazed saying, "What is this new teaching,
>   Even demonic spirits obey Him?"
The people went back to their homes telling everyone
>   About the mighty power and message of Jesus Christ.

Lord, I bow before Your omnipotent power.

Jesus Heals Peter's Mother-in-law and Others

Mark 1:29-45

Jesus left the synagogue and went to Peter's house
    Where his mother-in-law was sick with a fever.
When Jesus heard about it, He took her by the hand,
    Helped her up and the fever went away;
    She got up and prepared a meal for them.
At sundown the sick and demon-possessed
    Were brought to Peter's house for healing;
    The whole town crowded in to see what would happen.
Jesus cured many of them and cast demons out of others,
    But He wouldn't permit demons to speak
    Because they knew who He was.
In the morning, Jesus woke up before anyone else,
    And went into a private place to pray.
Simon and the others searched until they found Him,
    Then Peter said,
    "Master, everyone is looking for You."
Jesus told them He couldn't stay in Capernaum,
    But He said, "Let us go to the towns of Galilee
So I can preach to people there,
    That is why I came into the world."
As Jesus went through Galilee, a leper pleaded with Him,
    "If You are willing, You can heal me."
Because Jesus was moved with love for him, He touched the leper
    And said to him, "Be healed!"
    Immediately, his leprosy was healed.
Then Jesus sent him to be examined by a priest, and
    To make an offering that was required by Moses.
Jesus also told him not to tell anyone
    But the man told everyone what happened.
As a result, Jesus could no longer enter any town,

But even when He stayed in the fields,
People came to Him from all around.

Lord, I want You to touch me today,
*   To heal me of my sin and failure;*
Then let me touch You today
*   To experience Your victorious power.*

The Story of Getting a Friend to Jesus

Unbeknownst to the disciples of Jesus, more than just large crowds await-ed them in the city. Religious authorities in Jerusalem had sent represen-tatives to observe Jesus of Nazareth and report on his activities and teachings to the Sanhedrin. If possible, they were to entrap Jesus, to find something they could use to discredit Him as a teacher or even have Him arrested by the civil magistrates. So Pharisees and scribes of the Law had come to Capernaum from the neighboring towns of Galilee and from Jerusalem to scrutinize the so-called Messiah.

Early one morning, Jesus knocked at Peter's door, even though his friends knew that Simon Peter was a sound sleeper and a late riser. But this morn-ing, Peter was up, sitting at the breakfast table with Andrew.

"Come in," Peter motioned to Jesus. "Sit down and eat with us."

In short order, the room was filled with disciples. James and John had come from their father's home, telling people along the way that Jesus would be teaching this day. One by one, neighbors came to Peter's door asking, "May we come in? We want to hear what the rabbi says...."

The priest from the synagogue came to the house, and with him came vis-iting rabbis from Jerusalem and doctors of the Law from local villages. Because rabbis always occupied the places of honor, they sat near to Jesus, while everyone else was left to the other places in the room.

As usual, the majority of the listeners were responsive to Jesus' teaching. Some were just curious; others were hungry to know God. The religious leaders were not warm and responsive; doubt hung on their faces for all to see.

About the third hour of the day, down the main street of Capernaum came four men carrying a stretcher between them. On the stretcher was a friend, a paralytic man. They had started out before dawn from a town seven miles away, bringing their crippled friend to see Jesus. But when they reached the home of Peter and Andrew, they were unable to get to the front door. People were blocking the doorway.

"Please," the spokesman pleaded. "Let us through to see Jesus."

"Sh-h-h!" someone hushed them.

Picking up the bed with their friend, they went around to the back door, but again a crowd of people blocked the way into the building.

The four men lifted their paralytic friend and carried him up the stone stairs that led to the roof. No one took notice of them as they mounted the stairs; all attention was focused on what was going on inside the house. On the roof they found hard-packed dirt covering the flat stone tiles underneath. The four men began digging at the dirt with their hands. With a stick, they pried up a covering tile above the family room, and sunlight poured into the home of Peter.

"What are you doing?" Peter hollered, while his visitors shouted in protest against the loose dirt and pebbles raining down on them. Jesus raised a hand to hush the crowd.

The crowd was stunned to see the form of a man in a large blanket being lowered through the hole in the ceiling. Several men seated nearby stood to grab the pallet and assisted in lowering it slowly to the floor. The feverish face and glistening eyes of the paralyzed man turned up to Jesus.

Jesus said to the man, "Your sins are forgiven."

The Scribes and Pharisees in the room dared say nothing; they exchanged contemptuous looks, asking the same questions in their hearts and minds: Why does this man speak blasphemy? *Who can forgive sins but God?*

Then Jesus turned to the scribes and Pharisees and said to them, "Why are you thinking these things? Which is easier: To say to the paralytic, 'Your sins are forgiven,' or to say, 'Get up, take your bed and walk'?"

Peter suppressed a laugh. Jesus smiled and said, "But that you may know that the Son of Man has authority on earth to forgive sins...." Jesus then turned to the paralyzed man and said to him, "I tell you, get up, take your blanket and go home."

Immediately, the man stood up, gathered up his pallet and walked through the crowd and out the front door to the accompaniment of unabashed cheers and praises to God.

My Time To Pray

- Lord, I want to be a "helper" of needy people, getting them to Jesus.

- Lord, give me tenacity to seek Your presence when people or things block my access to You.

- Lord, give me faith to pray for sick people so they can get well.

Getting a Friend to Jesus

Matthew 9:1-8; Mark 2:1-12; Luke 5:18-20

Jesus was in Peter's house in Capernaum
>When a crowd gathered to hear Him teach,
>So that the house was packed with people.
Four men brought a man with palsy to Jesus
>But they could not get in the house
>Because there were so many people.

They took the sick man up to the roof,
>Then removed tiles in the roof,
>And let down the palsied man in front of Jesus.
Jesus knew they had faith for healing
>So He said, "Son, your sins are forgiven."
There were some Jewish leaders in the crowd
>Who criticized Jesus in their hearts, saying,
>"Who can forgive sins but God?
"This man is blaspheming God,
>Does He think He is God?"
Jesus knew their thoughts and said to them,
>"Why are you criticizing in your mind?
"What is easier to say, 'Your sins are forgiven';
>Or 'arise, pick up your bedroll and walk?'"
Then Jesus told them He would prove
>That He was the Messiah—the Son of Man,
>Who could forgive sins.
Jesus then told the man, "Get up, pick up
>Your bedroll and walk."
The man jumped to his feet, took his bedroll,
>And everyone saw him walk.
They were astounded and praised God saying,
>"We have never seen anything like this."

Lord, I praise You for the way
>*Jesus handled those who criticized Him.*
Lord, I am astounded at everything You do.

A Story of the Call to Matthew

The road from Damascus to Egypt ran outside the outer wall of Capernaum. Jesus and his disciples exited Capernaum through the city gate, turned left on the Roman road and began walking south in the direction of Judea.

Almost immediately, they encountered the customs booth where taxes were collected. Capernaum was the convergence of most traveled roads in Galilee, so that's where taxes were collected.

Everything that went through customs was taxed—grain, wine, cloth, produce of all kinds. To add to the burden, Levi, the chief tax collector for King Herod, collected *ad valorem* on everything that passed his table: axles, wheels, pack animals, and anything else he could think of to tax. Thus he had become extremely wealthy.

Because tax collectors ruled over everything that passed through their domains, they were thought to be oppressors. Rabbis expelled at once any Jew who accepted a job collecting taxes for the Romans.

Levi was philosophical about his ejection from the synagogue in Capernaum. But deep down he knew he was a sinful man. Levi had paid attention to the crowds listening intently to this new teacher.

When he looked up to see Jesus in the tax line, Levi wanted to say something to Him, but he didn't know how to greet Him. As Jesus stepped to Levi's table, Jesus said to him simply, "Follow Me."

With this simple invitation from Jesus, Levi saw his past swallowed up. And an overwhelming sense of relief washed over him.

Levi left the booth to follow Jesus.

Jesus looked behind him and smiled, saying, "You will be called Matthew, for you are a gift of God."

My Time To Pray

- Lord, may I instantaneously obey when Jesus enters my life and calls me to do a job.

- Lord, keep reminding me that there is no sinner who is too hardened to follow You as a dedicated disciple.

• Lord, teach me to love the unsaved, as You loved Matthew.

The Call to Matthew

Matthew 9:9-17; Mark 2:13-22; Luke 5:27-39

Jesus left Capernaum and followed the road
> That ran along side of the Sea of Galilee.

When Jesus came to the customs office,
> He saw Levi sitting there calculating taxes.

Jesus said to Him, "Follow me,"
> And to everyone's amazement,
> Levi left the tax office to follow Jesus.

That evening, Levi gathered a number of his friends
> To hear Jesus—politicians and tax collectors.

When the Jewish leaders saw Jesus eating with the crowd,
> They called His disciples,
> "Why does your master eat with questionable characters?"
> When Jesus knew what the religious leaders asked,
> He asked a question to get His point across,

"Do the healthy need a doctor, or
> Is it the sick who need help?

"I did not come to offer salvation to people
> Who think they are good enough,
> But I offer salvation to sinners."

The disciples of John the Baptist and the Jewish leaders fasted
> As part of their religious activities.

They approached Jesus, asking,
> "Why do these disciples of John the Baptist and Pharisees fast
> But Your disciples do not?"

Jesus answered, "Do you expect wedding guests to fast
> When they are at the wedding feast?

"They eat as long as they are with the bridegroom,
    But they will fast when the bridegroom
    Is taken from them."
Jesus continued, "No one sews a patch of unshrunken cloth
    On an old coat.
"If he does, the new patch will shrink and tear the old coat
    And it will be worse than ever.
"No one puts new wine into an old wineskin,
    As the new wine ferments, it will burst
    The old wine skin.
"The wine will be lost and the wineskin ruined."
    New challenges need new solutions.

Lord, teach me when to embrace the new,
    Guide me when to leave the old.

Chapter 7

My Father's House and Kingdom

The Story of Jesus Cleansing the Temple

When it was nearly time for the Jewish Passover, Jesus and his disciples made the journey to Jerusalem. Inside the temple, loud voices filled the courtyard. The Galileans had expected to hear Levites singing psalms. But instead of reverence, they saw a tumultuous crowd. People were buying and selling in the outer courtyard. Moneychangers were negotiating with worshipers to change foreign coins into Hebrew currency for temple offerings.

One farmer held several oxen by a harness. Another had a small pen for lambs. Still another had a gigantic bull he was trying to sell. "If you have a big sin, I have a big bull," he hollered.

Jesus' nostrils flared, He picked up three leather cords laying near Him on the ground. He walked up the stairs and out onto a small wall where He could be seen. Then, lifting His voice, He cried, *"How dare you turn my Father's house into a market! This is not a house of merchandise!"*

Laughter erupted from the businessmen.

"Stop!" Jesus yelled out over the crowd. Silence began to ripple out to the edges of the courtyard.

"This is a house of prayer," Jesus' voice echoed. "Take your business outside the temple. Now!"

There was absolute silence. No one moved.

The owner of the bull pointed at Jesus and shouted, "Why don't you take your business outside." He laughed at Jesus. The crowd that had been given over to unrestrained haggling now united in scorn.

Leaping down, Jesus kicked a table over with a thunderous crash. He unleashed His wrath on the moneychangers' tables, overturning each of them in succession. Coins flew every which way. Cages crashed to the ground as Jesus stormed through the courtyard, turtledoves and pigeons fluttering free.

With His makeshift whip in hand and His face flushed with anger, Jesus stepped toward the man with the bull. The man stumbled backward and the bull bolted toward the exit. Merchants and customers scattered like leaves.

The businessmen had escaped, but many honest worshipers were still there. They were stunned yet scared, not knowing what Jesus would do to them.

"My Father's house is to be a house of prayer," Jesus announced to them.

Slowly, priests began appearing in the courtyard. One by one they appeared. They surveyed the coins on the floor, the broken pens and the overturned tables.

One of the priests walked over to Jesus. "By what authority do you clear the temple?" he asked.

"The priests are the keepers of the temple," he said. The other priests nodded.

Jesus ignored them.

"Are you not Jesus of Nazareth?" he asked. Word had reached Jerusalem of a Galilean doing miracles with wine. "What miraculous sign can you show us to prove your authority to do this?" the priest asked.

"If you destroy this temple," Jesus said in answer, "I will raise it again in three days."

"It has taken 46 years to build this temple," the priest mockingly answered, "and you think you can rebuild it in three days?"

No one fully understood what Jesus meant. But Jesus spoke of His own death and resurrection, which He knew was coming. Jesus remained in Jerusalem for Passover. He continued teaching and performing miracles. The temple merchants stayed out of His way and for the rest of the week they kept their merchandise out of the temple.

My Time To Pray

- Lord, may I always be angry at religious hypocrisy and those who practice Christianity to make money.

- Lord, keep my motives pure when I enter a church-house of worship.

- Lord, it's easy for me to get angry; help me control my temper and to only be angry against the inappropriate things people do at inappropriate times.

- Lord, I accept the centrality of Your resurrection as the validity of my faith. That's because I know Christ is alive in my heart.

Jesus Cleanses the Temple

John 2:13-25

Lord, when the Passover came in the spring of A.D. 26,
    Jesus went up to Jerusalem with His disciples.
Jesus found people in the temple selling animals and birds
    For sacrifice—cattle, sheep and pigeons.
Money changers had set up tables to exchange foreign coins
    Into Hebrew money
    Because they had images of false gods.

Jesus made a whip out of some rope and
      Drove the animals out of the temple
      And overturned the tables of the moneychangers.
Jesus commanded, "Stop turning my Father's House
      Into a market to sell your sacrifices."
The disciples were amazed at His anger and said,
      "His devotion to the Lord's House
      Burns in Him like a fire."
The Jewish leaders challenged Jesus,
      "What miracle can You show us
      That gives You authority to do this?"
Jesus replied, "Destroy this temple,
      And I will raise it up in three days."
They said, "It has taken 46 years to build this temple,
      Do You think You can rebuild it in three days?"
After the resurrection His disciples remembered this event
      And realized Jesus was referring to
      Raising up His body, not rebuilding the temple.
While Jesus was in Jerusalem for the Passover,
      Many believed in Him because they saw
      The miracles He did.
But Jesus did not entrust Himself to them,
      Because He knew what was in their hearts.

Lord, come cleanse the temple of my heart,
      Just as You cleansed Herod's temple.

The Story of a Night Interview with Nicodemus

A cool breeze rustled the palm branches at the edge of the flat-roofed house. April was hot in the daytime but chilly at night. The Passover moon was so bright that the Torah could be read by its light. With no clouds in the sky, the stars created a perfect canopy for the evening discussion.

Jesus sat with John, James, and Peter on the rooftop, waiting for Nicodemus. A Jewish leader among the most influential in Jerusalem, Nicodemus would be severely censured by the Sanhedrin if they knew of this meeting. The other 69 members of the council did not consider Jesus to be a legitimate teacher. After all, Jesus had expelled the merchants from the temple; He was considered a menace.

But the taciturn shadows would hide all, the outside stairway allowing Nicodemus to slip upstairs unnoticed for his meeting with Jesus.

Passover week was a festive week for celebration. Many banquets were held during Passover. People got together to discuss current events, family matters, or just to renew old friendships. New friendships were also begun in this festive atmosphere. What began as a formal discussion would often end up in intimate conversation. This discussion between Jesus and Nicodemus was such an appointment, but Nicodemus wasn't ready to let his peers know about it, and Jesus understood this. Power...position...prestige...Nicodemus was a man with much to lose.

Young John had not said anything all evening. He was suspicious of priests, scribes, anyone who represented the religious establishment. Nicodemus was a Pharisee and a respected member of the Sanhedrin, the ruling council that exercised authority in all Jewish religious matters. The Roman governor was the final authority in Judean civil matters, but as part of the occupational agreement, the Romans allowed the Jews to take charge over their own religious and civil affairs—as long as they didn't interfere with the Roman government.

James gave voice to his brother's concerns. "Nicodemus is the most influential teacher in Jerusalem," he said. "He may have been sent here to spy on us."

But Jesus said nothing, and they waited.

When Nicodemus arrived with his academic attachés, he found two prominent chairs set on the roof, the first an ornate oak chair, padded with blue leather. This was the taller chair. Nicodemus would sit in the exalted chair, surrounded by his lieutenants. Across from him, a stool, lower in height, had been placed for Jesus. Behind Jesus was a bench set against the wall. On the bench sat John, the impulsive youth. Next to him was Peter, the stubborn, outspoken fisherman. Beside Peter sat James, the quiet but fiery one.

According to custom, it was the privilege of the elder Nicodemus to choose the topic of the evening. By all standards, it would have been inappropriate for Jesus to set the agenda for discussion. Nicodemus had a reputation for arguing the significance of historical events in the Talmud, those areas in which he excelled. Sometimes the discussions were nothing more than monologues, with Nicodemus discoursing all evening on a particularly fascinating topic. He was a brilliant scholar, and people invited him to their evening feasts just to glean something of his magnificent wisdom and understanding.

As they took their seats under the stars, Nicodemus and his three fellow scholars presented a formidable challenge for anyone wishing to engage in a religious debate. They held within their grasp a world of knowledge and learning that was feared by most illiterate people. Before them was Jesus, an itinerant teacher with no formal education, and three unlearned fishermen.

The disciples fully expected that the Pharisee would try to intimidate Jesus. But the shadows hid the face of Nicodemus, and his intentions were unclear. When at last he spoke, he did not attack Jesus, nor did he challenge Him with a question. Nicodemus leaned forward into the light, lowering his own head in clear deference to Jesus.

"We know about the miracles you have been doing in Jerusalem. We know about the miracle of turning water into wine...." Nicodemus' eyes were soft and pleading. They did not flash hot, nor were they ready for academic battle. "Rabbi, we know that you have come from God," he said, "because no one could perform these signs if God were not with Him."

To the disciples' surprise, Nicodemus had spoken to Jesus as an equal. Nicodemus, as the first to speak, had complimented Jesus. It was customary among such men that the compliment be returned.

Nicodemus waited for Jesus' reply. All eyes on the rooftop turned to Jesus who was sitting in the full moonlight. There were no shadows to hide

Jesus' reaction. Jesus waited for a few seconds to make sure it was His turn to speak. But rather than return the compliment, Jesus bypassed the niceties of rhetoric and went straight to the heart of the issue—the reason Nicodemus had come. Jesus told him, "Unless a man is born again, he cannot see the kingdom of Heaven."

The body language of three scholars-in-tow stiffened; they didn't like what they heard. They expected Jesus to compliment Nicodemus on his wisdom or his influence with the Sanhedrin. But Jesus was blunt.

Nicodemus did not take offense at the slight. It was as if Jesus had known what the Pharisee had come seeking, so He answered his unspoken question. But Nicodemus was puzzled by the logical impossibility. "How can a man be born when he is old?" he asked. "Surely he cannot enter a second time into his mother's womb to be born!"

"I tell you the truth, unless a person is born of water and of the Spirit, that person cannot enter the kingdom of God."

The three lieutenants to Nicodemus were disarmed by the intimacy of the discussion. Though offended when Jesus didn't compliment their leader, the warm, inquisitive response of Nicodemus told them the discussion was going well.

"Flesh gives birth to flesh, but the Spirit gives birth to spirit." Jesus explained, "When a man is born into this world that man is flesh, like the parents who gave him birth. But when a man is born of the Spirit, his life will be rooted in the spiritual."

Nicodemus understood the simplicity of Jesus' logic; there was a profundity in its simplicity. *But what does it mean to be "born again,"* he wondered silently.

Jesus looked deep into the eyes of Nicodemus. "You shouldn't be surprised when I tell you, 'You must be born again.'"

A swift evening breeze swept up the street and over the house. "Being born again is like the blowing of the wind," Jesus said to help Nicodemus. "You hear the sound of the wind, but you cannot tell where it comes from or where it is going. So it is with everyone born of the Spirit."

Nicodemus' eyes were still searching. Jesus continued. "Sometimes the wind stops blowing. Other times it blows briskly. No one can tell the wind where to blow, or when to blow. The wind blows wherever it pleases. So the world cannot fathom a man born of the Spirit."

"How can this be?" Nicodemus asked.

"You are Israel's teacher," Jesus said to Nicodemus. "You claim to know about God, and yet you have difficulty understanding the simplest teachings of the Kingdom."

Jesus arose from his stool and walked to the wall. Nicodemus followed him, listening as they walked. The others remained seated. Jesus looked out on the people in the street below. People were still walking, returning home from work or an evening meal. From the house next door there came the sound of congenial laughter. Everywhere Jesus looked, there were people who needed to hear about the kingdom of God.

Jesus turned to Nicodemus and said, "I have spoken to you of earthly things and you do not believe. Then how will you believe if I speak to you of heavenly things?"

Jesus folded His robe over His arm and returned to His stool. Beckoning to Nicodemus, He motioned for him to sit with the others. This was no longer a discussion between two great scholars, but a lesson from a master teacher.

"As Moses lifted up the serpent in the wilderness, so must the Son of Man be lifted up. Whoever looked at the snake on the pole, did not die of poison, and whoever believes in the Son of Man will live forever.

"For God so loved the world that He sent His only Son, that whoever believes in Him will not perish, but have everlasting life.

"For God did not send His Son into the world to condemn the world, but to save the world through Him. But whoever does not believe stands condemned already because he has not believed in the name of God's one and only Son."

Nicodemus did not know what to say to this.

"God has sent His Son as a light into the world..., Jesus explained. Just then a cloud covered the moon. The rooftop went black, as though a cosmic hand had extinguished its light. Almost immediately with the blackness, they heard a wicked laugh from the shadows in the street below...a chilling laughter.

The scholars and the disciples traded glances. Jesus, sensing the moment, said, "Men love darkness rather than light because their deeds are evil and the darkness hides what they are doing. But he who lives according to the truth will come into the light, that his deeds may be clearly seen, that they have been done in the name of God."

Nicodemus nodded. A spark had been touched in his own soul, and he determined to do whatever he could within the Sanhedrin to allow Jesus to teach openly. And Nicodemus himself would watch...and listen.

My Time To Pray

- Lord, come into my heart and save me, I want to be born again (pray this if you are not a Christian).

- Lord, help me be an example to my family and friends who are not born again so they can become Christians.

- Lord, take away any blindness that keeps me from seeing the truth of the new birth.

A Night Interview With Nicodemus

John 3:1-21

Nicodemus was a Jewish leader who observed the Law;
  He came to Jesus at night to compliment Him, saying,
"Jesus, You are a Teacher who comes from God

Because You perform miracles
That couldn't be done without God's help."
Jesus told him, "Verily, verily, I say to you,
You must be born again
To see the kingdom of God."
Nicodemus replied, "How can a man be born
When he is old? Can he go back
Into his mother's womb to be born again?"
Jesus answered, "Verily, verily, I say to you,
Unless you are born again of water and the Spirit,
You will not enter the kingdom of God.
"That which is born of flesh is flesh,
That which is born of Spirit is Spirit.
"Do not be surprised when I tell you,
'You must be born again.'
"The wind blows anywhere it pleases;
You can hear its sound, but you
Cannot tell where it comes from or goes.
"That describes those who are born of the Spirit,
And how the Spirit bestows life on them."
Nicodemus asked, "How can this happen?"
Jesus answered, "You are a respected teacher,
Yet you do not understand these things."
Jesus continued, "Verily, verily, I say to you,
I am telling you what I know,
But you will not believe me."
"If you do not believe what I say about this world,
How can you believe heavenly things?
"Since I have come to earth from Heaven,
I can explain heavenly things to you.
"As Moses lifted up the serpent in the wilderness,
So people could repent by looking to the serpent.
"In the same way the Son of Man will be lifted up

So that everyone who believes in Him will be saved.
"The Father loved everyone in the world so much
　　That He gave His only begotten Son
　　To die for each of them.
"So that everyone who believes in the Son
　　Will not perish in hell,
　　But will have eternal life.
"For the Father did not send His Son
　　To condemn the people of the world
　　But that they might be saved through Him.
"No one who believes in the Son will be condemned,
　　But those who refuse to believe in the name
　　Of God's only Son are condemned already."

The verdict of death is handed down because light
　　Has shined to the people of the world,
But people love darkness more than light
　　Because of their love of evil things.
Everyone who continually does evil things
　　Hates the light and rejects it
　　Because it exposes their motives and actions.

Lord, I want everyone to know that You offer eternal life
　　When Jesus told Nicodemus, "You can be born again."

Lord, I want to live by Your truth
　　So I will come into the light
　　So everyone can see what I do for You.

Jesus and John the Baptist

John 3:22-36

Jesus and His disciples left Jerusalem for the countryside
　　Where many people were baptized by His disciples.

John the Baptist was baptizing nearby at Aenon;
    Many also came there for baptism.
The Jewish leaders tried to tell the disciples of John the Baptist
    That the baptism of Jesus
    Was better than their baptism.
John's disciples came to tell Him, "The man
    You baptized—the one you called Messiah—
    He is baptizing more than you are."
John the Baptist answered, "God in Heaven
    Gives each man the work he is to do,
I told you I am not the Messiah, I am sent
    To prepare the way for Messiah.
"The crowds—the Bride of Christ—will naturally
    Go where Christ the Bridegroom is located.
"I am a friend of the bridegroom, I rejoiced
    When I answered His voice calling to me.
"He—Jesus—must increase,
    I—John the Baptist—must decrease.
"He comes from Heaven, and He is greater than all;
    We who are born on this earth
    Only understand the things of earth."
"Those who believe in Jesus have discovered
    The truth of God that has come from Heaven.
"He speaks the words of God
    Because He has the Spirit of God on Him.
"The Father loves Jesus, the Son,
    And has given everything to Him."

Lord, I believe in the Son, I have eternal life;
    Those who refuse to believe in the Son,
Will never have eternal life;
    But Your punishment rests on them.

The Story of the Samaritan Woman

John 4:1-42

As the scorching April sun neared its zenith, the disciples trudged up yet another charred Samaritan hill. Jesus had been led by the Holy Spirit to make the difficult trek through Samaria on their return home from Jerusalem.

"If we had gone by way of the Jordan Valley," young John complained, "we could have avoided these hills and saved ourselves a few blisters."

"Ha!" Peter laughed. With his lighter complexion, his red eyebrows were beginning to blend into a sunburned face. "I don't mind how we get there, as long as we're heading home," he said, keeping in mind that his Master had chosen this route. "Let's not complain…."

John pointed to the sun directly overhead. "It's nearly noon. We need to stop and let Jesus rest."

"The village of Sychar is up ahead."

"Jacob's Well is closer," John reminded him. "Let's stop there."

Jesus looked to John as though he could go no farther. Several days of intense ministry to the people in Jerusalem had seemed to drain Him. Peter gave Jesus a needed shoulder to lean on. The small olive trees surrounding the well were in sight just a few paces up the road.

Jacob's Well was located in the middle of the broad, flat valley with wheat growing in the fields on either side of the road. The fields were flanked by two mountains rising several hundred feet from the desert floor, forming a beautiful backdrop. To the disciples' left was Mount Ebal, the Mount of Blessings, where Joshua had once sacrificed to the Lord for the great victory over the northern kingdom. To their right was Mount Gerizim, the Mount of Cursing. The mountains stood like sentinels guarding the deep well that had been dug by Jacob, the father of the 12 tribes of Israel.

Now the area was populated with Samaritans, and most Jews had very little to do with the Samaritans because of their apostate faith. Still, the Jews revered the well of their forefather and would make the pilgrimage to this place just to drink from the well and pray to the God of Jacob.

Jesus wearily collapsed onto the stone wall next to the well, under the shade of a small olive tree, where He promptly fell asleep.

"Let's go into town and get something to eat," Andrew said to John. "No one will bother Jesus. It's too hot to come for water at this hour of the day." So the disciples left their Master sleeping by the well, and they made their way to Sychar.

Jesus was dozing in the shade and didn't hear the bare feet coming down the powdery road toward the well. He sat up when he heard the squeak of a leather bucket being lowered into the well. A Samaritan woman was there. She wore dark clothes—a black robe similar to that of a widow or an unmarried woman. A dark blue shawl protected her from the sun.

"Oh...," she said, startled by the presence of a stranger at the well. She let go of the rope and her bucket fell with a distant splash a moment later. "I didn't see you resting in the shade."

Jesus greeted her kindly, then seeing her jar asked, "Could you give Me something to drink? I am very thirsty."

"But you are a Jew and I am a Samaritan woman," the woman said, her curiosity winning out over fear and hatred. Looking past their cultural differences, she knew it was highly unusual for a Jewish man to talk alone with a woman. And yet there was something different about this man.

"How can you ask me for a drink?" she demanded.

Jesus did not immediately answer.

"Jews have no dealings with the Samaritans," she reminded Him.

Jesus was not interested in such distinctions. He was, however, interested in the life of this woman. He knew she was why the Holy Spirit had led Him and His disciples into the hills of Samaria.

"If only you knew the gift of God," He said, smiling at her reluctance. "If you knew who it was that asked you for a drink, you would ask for water from Me. Anyone who drinks from My living water will never thirst again."

"Where would you get this 'living water'? Sir, you have no bucket. You have no rope, and the well is deep."

Jesus continued to smile at her.

"Who are you?" the woman asked. "Are you greater than our father Jacob who gave us this well and drank from it, as did his sons, his flock and his herds?"

"Everyone who drinks this water will be thirsty again," Jesus answered, "but whoever drinks the water I offer will never thirst. Indeed, the water I give you will become in you a spring of water filling your heart and over-flowing into eternal life."

"I want this water," the woman said, "so that I don't have to come to this well to draw water again. I want eternal water."

"Go call your husband," Jesus said to the woman. "Tell your husband about the water of eternal life, then bring your husband here to see Me."

"I don't have a husband."

"I know you are telling me the truth," Jesus said to her, "for you have had five husbands in your lifetime, and the man you are now living with is not your husband."

Stunned, she said nothing for a moment. She had never met this man. How could He know all about her life? Her closest friends in Sychar did not know of her five marriages. She blurted out, "Sir, you must be a prophet of God. You know the secret things about me."

So she tested Him to learn whether he was indeed a prophet. "The Samaritans worship on Mount Gerizim where Joshua worshiped," she said, "but the Jews say we should worship in Jerusalem...."

Jesus had not come to argue religion with the Samaritan woman, so He didn't answer her.

"Where should we worship?" she asked.

"Woman, the hour is coming when you will not worship on a mountain or in Jerusalem. A time is coming when true worshipers will worship the Father in Spirit and in truth.... These are the kind of people the Father seeks to worship Him."

She did not have an answer for this, but said to Jesus, "I know the Messiah is coming. When He comes, He will explain everything to us."

"I who speak to you am the Messiah."

When the disciples returned with food and found Jesus talking with the Samaritan woman, they were taken aback but said nothing out of respect for their teacher. Nevertheless, the woman turned and ran swiftly away, leaving behind her water jar, rope, and bucket.

"Wait...!" Peter yelled after her, but she continued running.

The disciples drew water for Jesus and gave Him a drink from Jacob's Well. Unfolding their food cloth, they began distributing bread and dried lamb for lunch. But Jesus didn't eat.

Finally, Peter spoke. "Take some bread, Rabbi."

But Jesus shook His head and said, "I have food that you know nothing about."

The disciples looked at one another, wondering who could have brought Jesus food while they were gone.

When He saw His disciples wondering at His words, Jesus said to them, "My food is to do the will of my Father who sent Me and to finish His work." Jesus drew His strength from feeding others, as He had done for the Samaritan woman.

"Don't say there are yet four months until harvest," He said to them, pointing. "Lift up your eyes and look on the fields now." But Jesus wasn't pointing toward the wheat fields.

The disciples looked toward the village. Coming down the road from Sychar were dozens of men—all in white turbans—walking fast toward the well, looking like a field of whitened wheat waving in the wind.

Jesus said, "The field is white for harvest."

The woman had gone back to the city, babbling to everyone she knew, "Come see a man who told me everything I ever did." She ran from one group of men to another. To each group she said the same thing: "This man is from God."

Upon hearing about the man who knew the secrets of the heart, many Samaritans quickly ran out of Sychar toward Jacob's Well. They listened to Jesus and urged Him to stay with them. So Jesus and His disciples departed the well and went into Sychar.

That evening in the town piazza, Jesus taught the crowd from the Scriptures concerning himself. Many believed that He was the Christ. As He finished speaking, an elderly man stood, his stringy beard bouncing from his chin as he talked, "Now we believe You are the Messiah. We have heard for ourselves, and we believe You are the Savior of the world."

My Time To Pray

- Lord, make me thirsty for a drink from You.

- Lord, give me a passion to share my testimony with needy people like the Samaritan woman.

- Lord, I will tell my non-Christian friends, "Come see a Man who knows everything about me."

The Samaritan Woman

John 4:1-42

When Jesus left the Passover at Jerusalem,
    He surprisingly went home through Samaria
    Because the Jews have no dealings with the Samaritans.
When He came near Sychar, He sat on Jacob's well

Because He was worn out from the hot journey
And it was 12 noon.
The disciples went into the town to get food;
Jesus was sitting there when a Samaritan woman
Came to draw water from the well.
Jesus said, "Give me a drink";
She was surprised that a Jew
Would ask because the Jews despised the Samaritans.
She said, "Why would you—a Jew—ask water
From me, a Samaritan?"
Jesus said, "If you only knew God's gift
And Who it is that offers you water,
You would have asked Me for a drink,
And I would have given you living water.
The woman replied, "You do not have a bucket;
How could You get water from this deep well?"
She continued, "Are You greater than Jacob who drank
From this well with his family and cattle
Then gave us this well?"
Jesus answered, "Whoever drinks this water
Will get thirsty again,
But those who drink of the water that I give
Will never be thirsty again.
"The water I give will be an artesian well inside them
That gushes up into eternal life."
The woman said, "Give me some of that water
So I will never get thirsty again,
And have to come to this well for water."
Jesus abruptly said, "Go call your husband!"
She answered, "I have no husband."
Jesus replied, "You have correctly answered
Because you have had five husbands."
"And now you're not married

To the one you're living with."
She exclaimed, "You must be a prophet to know this";
    Then she argued, "Our fathers worshiped here.
    The Jews say Jerusalem is the place to worship."
Jesus interrupted to say, "The hour is coming when no one will
    Worship on this mountain or in Jerusalem.
"You don't know whom you worship;
    The Jews know whom they worship.
"In fact, the hour is already here when true worshipers
    Will worship the Father in Spirit and truth.
"God is Spirit, and those who worship Him
    Must worship in spirit and truth."
The woman said, "I know that Messiah is coming;
    He will tell us everything when He comes";
    Jesus answered, "I am the Messiah."

Lord, the disciples were surprised when they returned
    Because Jesus was talking to a Samaritan woman.

The woman left her water pot and hurried off
    To tell the men in the village,
"Come see a man who told me
    Everything I've ever done."
She asked, "Could this man be the Messiah?"
    They left the town to go meet Jesus.
Meanwhile, the disciples told Jesus to eat
    But He said, "I have food to eat
    That you don't know about."
The disciples thought somene else had
    Brought Him food.
Jesus said, "My food is doing the will of the Father
    And completing His work.
"People say, 'Harvest comes four months after planting,'
    "But I say, 'Look around at the fields

They are already ripe for harvest.'
"Everything is ready for the reaper to go to work
    To bring in the 'grain' of eternal life;
    Then sower and reaper will rejoice together."
Then Jesus explained, "One sows, another reaps;
    I send you to reap where you didn't sow,
    And you get rewards for their effort."

Many Samaritans believed in Jesus
    Because the woman said, "Come see a man who
    Told me everything I have ever done."
The Samaritans begged Jesus to stay with them
    And He stayed two days,
    And many got saved.
The Samaritan men told the woman, "Now we believe
    Because of what we have heard for ourselves,
    Not just because of what you said."

Lord, thank You for saving the woman at the well,
    And thank You for saving me.

Healing the Nobleman's Son

John 4:43-54

Jesus returned to Cana where He turned water to wine,
    There an official from Herod's court
    Came begging Jesus to heal his son.
The official had sought to find Jesus in the area
    Because his son was very, very sick.
Jesus said, "Why is it that none
    Will believe in Me unless they see miracles?"
The official answered, "Come down to Capernaum
    And heal my son before he dies."

Jesus answered, "Go home, your son will live";
    The official believed the words of Jesus
    And turned to start his journey home.
While he was on the road, his servants met him
    To say, his son recovered.
The official asked what time had the fever broke;
    The servant told him, "4 P.M."
The father realized that was the same hour
    When Jesus said, "Your son will live."
This was the second sign-miracle Jesus did in Cana
    And the official and his family believed in Jesus.

The Story of Jesus Facing Unbelief in Nazareth

Word had spread quickly through the small village. The son of Mary and Joseph had returned to Nazareth and had been asked to speak at the synagogue.

Jesus entered the synagogue and took a seat reserved for visiting speakers. When the time came for Him to speak, the leader of the synagogue selected the writings of Isaiah, and handed the scroll to Jesus. Jesus carefully unrolled the scroll to where Isaiah prophesied concerning the Messiah, then read aloud:

> "The Spirit of the Lord is upon Me, because He has anointed Me to preach the gospel to the poor; He has sent Me to heal the brokenhearted, to proclaim liberty to the captives and recovery of sight to the blind, to set at liberty those who are oppressed; to proclaim the acceptable year of the Lord."

Jesus rolled the scroll back into place and returned it to the leader. Then He sat down. Every eye in the room looked at Him. They were waiting for His sermon.

But all Jesus said was, "Today this Scripture is fulfilled in your hearing."

The elders began to shake their heads in disapproval. The passage Jesus had read referred to the coming Messiah. The word that jumped to their minds was blasphemy, but no one wanted to say that word. This was Joseph's son.

"No!" one of the elders dared to say out loud. "You may be a worker of miracles, but You cannot call Yourself Messiah!" Jesus knew they came to see miracles but they did not believe in Him.

He said, "Many of you want Me to do miracles here in Nazareth as I have done at Capernaum and at Jerusalem. But I say to you, no prophet is accepted in his hometown."

The minister of the synagogue asked, "Why will You not show us what You can do? If You are the Messiah, give us a sign."

Jesus didn't answer him directly, but spoke to the congregation: "*In the time of Elisha, there were many lepers in Israel, but none of them were cleansed except Naaman, a Syrian. I cannot do miracles in my hometown because of your unbelief. You will not believe that I am who I say I am.*"

The synagogue erupted in indignation. Jesus had told them they were not fit for miracles.

Voices began to swell like thunder, and the Nazarenes drove Jesus out of their synagogue. They cursed Him and forced Him to the outskirts of town.

Just outside Nazareth, the road to Capernaum passed dangerously close to a 40-foot cliff. They pushed Jesus up the hill toward the cliff, determined to throw Him off. Jesus allowed Himself to be pressed forward until they reached the brow of the hill.

Then He turned and looked upon His pursuers, and the mob was silenced. They held their collective breath, waiting for Jesus to speak. But Jesus said nothing. He walked back down the hill toward Capernaum, His new home.

My Time To Pray

- Lord, may I be a good testimony to those who grew up with me.

- Lord, teach me how to properly react to those who are blinded with unbelief.

- Lord, there are people in this world who hate You and reject You; protect me when they attack me.

- Lord, I'm willing to be a martyr and die for You because You died for me.

- Lord, give me faith to pray for spiritual insight for those who are spiritually blinded.

Jesus Facing Unbelief in Nazareth

Luke 4:14-30

Jesus came back to minister in His home region, Galilee,
    And the power of the Holy Spirit was on Him.
Everyone in the region heard about Jesus
    And when He preached in the synagogues,
    Everyone was glad to hear Him.
Then Jesus went to Nazareth, His boyhood home,
    Because it was His custom on the Sabbath
    He went to the synagogue.
An elder handed Jesus the scroll of Isaiah,
    He unrolled it to a certain place and read,
"The Spirit of the Lord is upon Me,
    Because the Lord has anointed Me
    To preach the Gospel to the poor.
"The Lord has sent Me to preach prisoners shall be free,

And the blind shall see,
And the oppressed shall be released.
"*To proclaim, God will bless*
Those who come to Him."
Then Jesus rolled up the scroll
And returned it to its place
And took His seat.
Every eye in the synagogue stared at Him,
Then Jesus spoke,
"This Scripture was fulfilled today."
And everyone was amazed at what He said,
They said, "Is not this Joseph's Son?"
Jesus told them, "You will probably want me
To prove Myself, like the proverb,
'Physician, heal yourself.'
"You want Me to do miracles here in Nazareth
Like I have done in Capernaum
"But I know your unbelief,
You have not accepted Me,
But rather you have rejected Me.
"Verily, I say that no prophet
Is accepted in His hometown.
"Remember how Elijah did a miracle
To help the widow of Zerephath,
Even though she was a foreigner?
"There were many needy widows in Israel
Because there was a famine.
"It hadn't rained for three and a half years,
Yet, Elijah was not sent to them.
"Elijah also healed Naaman of leprosy
Even though there were many lepers in Israel."
The people in the synagogue were furious
When they heard what Jesus said.

The people mobbed Jesus and pushed Him outside
    Toward the edge of the cliff near town.
But He walked through the midst of the mob
    And returned to Capernaum.

Lord, give me the boldness of Jesus to face unbelief,
    And give me the wisdom of Jesus to do what is right.

Chapter 8

Jesus Heals

The Story of Healing at the Pool of Bethesda

When Jesus returned to Jerusalem to observe the Feast of Passover, He had gained popularity with the people. His reputation with the religious authorities had worsened, however.

Slowly Jesus eased through the crowd at the Pool of Bethesda, looking from one face to the next. Then, seeing a man against a wall, Jesus walked straight toward him.

The poor man's worn pallet showed the wear and tear of being rolled and unrolled every day for 38 years. Each day during that time, the lame man had waited in vain for the moving of the waters, knowing full well that when the waters were stirred he could not be first in.

The man slumped against the wall, his hope long depleted. In an act of rebellion against God nearly four decades earlier, the lame man had done something to make him crippled. Because of one act of rebellion, he had never walked again.

"Do you want to be healed?" Jesus asked.

"Sir, I don't have anyone to help me into the pool."

Jesus commanded the lame man, "Rise! Pick up your mat and walk."

Instantly, the man felt sensations he hadn't felt for 38 years. He stood! No one around him noticed, and he did not yell, scream, or dance. He had been told to take up his mat and walk, so he obeyed.

Jesus continued walking through the crowd. Because all eyes were fixed on the water, none had seen the miracle.

But a pair of Jewish leaders walking to the temple immediately spotted the healed man. "THIS IS THE SABBATH DAY!" they shouted. "PUT THAT MAT DOWN!"

The Sabbath day had been instituted as a sign of God's covenant with His people. Just as God rested from His work on the seventh day, so the Jews were to work six days and rest on the seventh. But through the years Jewish leaders had developed so many regulations, the meaning of the Sabbath had become hopelessly obscured.

Now inside the temple, the lame man who was healed wanted to say to God, "Thank you for healing me."

Suddenly, Jesus was there. "God has heard your prayers," Jesus said.

The healed man's eyes welled up with tears of gratitude.

But Jesus did not seek the man's gratitude, He sought his heart. He searched the man's eyes. "Do not go back to the sin that crippled you."

Then Jesus turned and melted into the crowd.

Unknown to the man, the Pharisees had been watching. They had recognized Jesus, and approached the man.

"Was that the man who healed you?" they demanded. The healed man nodded.

"Did He tell you to pick up your bed and walk?" "Yes."

Immediately the priests stormed through the crowds after Jesus. Not only had He healed the lame man but He had incited the man to break the Sabbath! They finally caught up to Jesus near the Gate Beautiful. "Why do You violate the Sabbath?"

Jesus smiled a knowing smile and nodded His head. He said to them, "My Father is always ready to work on the Sabbath day, and so the Son must work while He is on earth."

"Blasphemy!" a priest shouted. Jesus had proclaimed himself the Son of God.

By now a large crowd was gathering, drawn by the shouting. If they had been outside the temple, the crowd would have stoned Jesus. Jesus saw the rage in their hearts, but said,

"I tell you the truth, the Son can do nothing by Himself. He can do only what He sees His Father doing. For the Father loves the Son and shows Him all things. You have never heard His voice nor seen His form, nor does His Word dwell in you, for you do not believe the One He sent."

The priests retired to discuss what they had just heard, and to plot how they could put Jesus to death.

My Time To Pray

- Lord, help me not give excuses as the lame man.

- Lord, see me in the middle of a crowd as You saw the lame man and come help me today.

- Lord, take away any hardness of my heart as the Jewish leaders rejected You. Help me respond positively to Your direction for my life.

The Lame Man at Bethesda

John 5:1-17

Jesus obeyed the Old Testament command to attend
    The Feast of Passover at Jerusalem
    At the end of His first full year of ministry.
Jesus went by the pool of Bethesda, a name

That meant "House of Mercy."
There were five porches where a great number
Of sick invalids were waiting
For an angel to come stir the waters in the pool.
The sick believed that the first one into the water
Would automatically get healed.
There was a man who had waited unsuccessfully for 38 years;
Jesus went only to him because
He had been there a long time.
Jesus asked, "Would you like to be healed?"
The lame man answered, "I don't have anyone
To put me in the waters after it is stirred up.
"When I am going to the water,
Someone jumps in before me."
Jesus said, "Take up your bedroll and walk";
Immediately, the man was healed
And he picked up his bedroll and walked.
The healed man walked through the crowd to the temple;
The Jews told him it was wrong
To carry any burden—a bedroll—on the Sabbath.
The lame man answered that the One who healed him
Also told him to pick up his bedroll.
Later Jesus found the healed man in the temple
And told him, "Go and don't do the sin any more
That was responsible for this lame condition; because
A worse thing will happen if you do."
The healed man went and told the Jews
That it was Jesus who healed him.

Equal in Nature, Power, and Authority

John 5:18-30

The Jews confronted Jesus
> Because He told the healed man
> To carry his bedroll on the Sabbath.
Jesus answered the Jewish leaders, "My Father
> Has worked up until now, now I work."
The Jewish leaders sought to kill Jesus because
> Jesus said He was just like the Father,
> And because He had broken their law,
> And He said the Father and Son are equal in nature.

Jesus answered the Jewish leaders, "Verily, verily,
> I say to you, the Son does nothing by Himself.
"But when the Son sees the things the Father does,
> He does the same things."
> The Father and Son are equal in power.

Then Jesus said, "The Father loves the son
> And shows the Son everything He does.
"The Father will do greater miracles
> Than healing the lame so you'll marvel.
"As the Father raises the dead and gives them life,
> So the Son will also raise the dead."
> The Father and Son are equal in authority.

"The Father does not judge the sins of everyone,
> All judgment is given to the Son;
> He that honors not the Son, honors not the Father."
"Verily, verily," Jesus said, "he that receives My Word,
> And believes on Me, has eternal life.
"That one will not be judged for his sins
> But has passed from death unto eternal life."

"Verily, verily," Jesus said, "the time is coming
>When all dead will hear My voice
>And be raised to eternal life.
"The Father has given Me the authority to execute judgment;
>Therefore, the time is coming when all in the grave
>Will hear My voice and be raised.
"They who have obeyed the Father will be raised
>To the resurrection of life.
"They who have disobeyed the Father will be raised
>To the resurrection of the damned."
Jesus told them, "I can do nothing by Myself,
>But I do the will of the Father who sent Me."

Four Witnesses: John the Baptist, Jesus' Miracles, the Father's Voice, and the Scriptures

John 5:31-47

Jesus said, "No one can bear witness of themselves
>And have other people believe them.
"The Old Testament said at the mouth of two witnesses
>Shall every testimony be established.
"The testimony of John the Baptist was a light
>That shined so people believed what he said about Me."

"But the testimony of My miracles was even greater;
>They proved the Father sent Me into the world."

"A third testimony is the voice of the Father that
>Thundered at My baptism. No one has seen God,
>But you heard His voice but didn't believe it.
"Because you do not have the Word of God dwelling in you,
>You do not believe the words the Father said."

116

Jesus told them, "Search the Scriptures, these words
      Testify of Me that I am from the Father.
"You think you have eternal life but you don't
      Because you refuse to believe in Me;
      You do not have the love of God in you."
Jesus said, "I have come in the Father's name,
      And you will not receive Me
      Yet you receive others coming in their own name.
"You seek glory from other Jewish leaders
      And do not seek the glory that comes
      From the heavenly Father.
"I will not accuse you in the final judgment
      Moses whom you revere;
      He will accuse you in the judgment.
"If you believe Moses—and you don't—then
      You would believe Me
      Because Moses predicted my coming."

"The Lord your God will raise up to you a prophet
From your brothers who will be like me (Moses). *Listen to Him"*
(Deut. 18:15).

Lord, I receive the four testimonies and believe them.
      Jesus, You are God and I worship You.

Debate About the Sabbath

Matthew 12:1-8; Mark 2:23-28; Luke 6:1-5

As Jesus journeyed home from the Passover at Jerusalem
      He went past the corn fields on the Sabbath
      And His disciples picked the grain and ate it.
The Pharisees criticized them because
      They broke the Sabbath Law.

Jesus answered that David went into the Tabernacle
        To eat the shewbread when he was hungry
        And those with him also ate it.
Jesus also mentioned the priest ate shewbread
        On the Sabbath day which outwardly broke the Law.
Then Jesus added Hosea the prophet said,
        "God wants us to be merciful,
        He doesn't want us to just to keep the Law.
"God wants us to know Him,
        Not just bring burnt sacrifices to Him."
Finally Jesus noted, "The Sabbath was made
        To serve man, not for man to just keep its law."
Jesus proclaimed, "Therefore the Son of Man
        Is master of the Sabbath, not the reverse."

Lord, help me properly observe Your Lord's Day,
        Not as the religious leaders legalistically observed it.
        Lord, I will worship You properly on Sunday.

The Shriveled Hand Healed

Matthew 12:10-14; Mark 3:1-5; Luke 6:6-11

When Jesus got to Capernaum He entered the synagogue,
        And a man was there with a shriveled up hand.
The Jewish leaders watched Jesus closely
        Whether He would heal on the Sabbath day
        So they could charge Him with breaking the Law.
Jesus said to the man with the shriveled up hand,
        "STAND IN THE MIDDLE OF PEOPLE."
Then Jesus asked, "Is it right to
        Help or hurt on the Sabbath Day?
        To kill or save lives?"
        Jesus continued, "If a man's sheep fall into a pit,

Isn't it proper to rescue the sheep on a Sabbath day?
Isn't a man worth more than a sheep?"
But the Pharisees wouldn't answer Jesus,
He looked at them with anger,
Being grieved for their hardness of heart.
Jesus then said to the man,
"STRETCH OUT YOUR HAND."
The man held out this withered hand
And it was completely restored.
And the Jewish leaders refused to believe in Him,
But began making plans to destroy Jesus.

Lord, I don't want to be critical of anyone
Who comes to You for help or healing
Like the Jewish leaders criticized You.

Lord, I marvel at Your compassion on
Those who hurt or need Your help;
And at Your patience with those who reject You.

Multitudes Healed

Matthew 12:15-16; Mark 3:7-12; Luke 6:17-19

Jesus and His disciples left to go to the seaside;
Multitudes followed Him from Galilee, Judea,
Jerusalem, Idumea, Tyre, and Sidon.
Because they heard about His miracles.
Jesus told His disciples to have a boat ready,
Because the crowds were crushing Him.
Jesus had cured so many people that anyone
With an ailment crowded in to touch Him.
When people possessed with demons encountered Jesus,
They fell down at His feet screaming,

"You are the Son of God."
But Jesus warned them repeatedly
That they should not make Him known.

Lord, Your healing power demonstrates
You are a powerful God,
Your tenderness demonstrates You are a loving God.

The Story of Choosing the Twelve Apostles

Knowing the religious authorities plotted against His life, Jesus withdrew with His disciples to the Sea of Galilee. A great multitude followed.

The crowds pressed in on Jesus so much, He was unable to talk with His disciples. He asked that a small boat be kept ready to take Him across the sea should the crowd grow unruly.

Jesus climbed into the boat and sailed away, leaving the crowd on shore. Arriving near Magdala, He left the craft on the beach and climbed a steep hill, looking for a place where He could be alone. Tonight, Jesus would ask His heavenly Father for guidance to appoint 12 as His followers or apostles.

All those who faithfully followed Him were known as His "disciples," but Jesus would call His chosen 12 "apostles," a Greek word that meant "sent ones." The 12 apostles would be the ones He would send to carry the Gospel, or good news, to the entire earth.

Jesus prayed all night. When the sun peeked over the eastern mountains, He came down from the hill to where the disciples were waiting.

Jesus said to them. "All of you will continue to follow Me. You will all be called disciples. But only 12 will be apostles. They will preach and be given power to heal sickness and cast out demons."

Jesus looked from face to face. "Simon will be first," Jesus nodded to the strapping fisherman. "Simon will be called Peter, for he will be strong."

His next choice was James. Everyone was surprised by this choice, because James was so quick to anger. The third choice was his brother John, the youngest of all the disciples.

Jesus said, "James and John are as thunder; they will roar like the thunderstorm at sin or iniquity."

Jesus selected Andrew as his fourth apostle. Once a follower of John the Baptist, Andrew was sensitive to the needs of people. "Philip, you too will be an apostle. Philip will be in charge of the next three apostles and will supervise the crowds, arrange accommodations, and other details."

Jesus appointed three other apostles to serve with Philip: his friend Nathanael; Matthew, the former tax collector; and Thomas, who was known for his pragmatism.

"The ninth apostle will be James, son of Alphaeus," Jesus nodded to the shortest of His disciples. "Your group will be in charge of our money."

To work with James, Jesus called Thaddeus and Simon the Zealot.

The first 11 men Jesus chose were from Galilee. They spoke with a Galilean accent, and understood the area from which Jesus came.

Then Jesus announced, "Judas Iscariot will be my twelfth apostle. He is the one especially chosen by My Father." He assigned Judas to carry the money bag.

Choosing the Twelve

Matthew 10:1-4; Mark 3:13-20; Luke 6:12-16

Jesus went up into the hill country
    And He continued all night in prayer.
The next day He called certain men to be His apostles
    So they would be with Him to learn,
Then they would be sent forth to preach,
    Heal and cast out demons.

Simon was the first whom He called Peter,
    He was the leader of the first group of four.
That included James and John
    Whom Jesus named the Sons of Thunder
    And Andrew was in that group.
The second group of four apostles was led by Philip,
    And included, Bartholomew, Matthew
    And Thomas, the one with a twin brother.
The third group of four was led by James the short one,
    And included, Thaddeus and Simon
The former terrorist fighter and Judas Iscariot,
    The one who betrayed Jesus.

Lord, teach me to pray about important decisions,
    As You prayed before choosing the 12 disciples.

Chapter 9

THE SERMONS OF JESUS

The Story of the Sermon on the Mount

The morning broke softly over the hills around Tiberias. Jesus left the highway and began to climb. He pointed to the top of a small hill.

"Up there," he said.

At the pinnacle of the hill, the mount flattened out and Jesus sat on a rock with His disciples. This was the place Jesus would hold His first staff meeting. Jesus would use this sermon to instruct His disciples about their attitude and actions as they served Him.

But they were not alone. The multitudes had followed Jesus. Every day, more and more people were coming to be near Him. They wanted to know what Jesus would do about re-establishing David's earthly kingdom. So the disciples sat close to Jesus as the multitude spread out on the mountain to hear this, "The Sermon on the Mount."

The Sermon on the Mount

Matthew 5:1–7:29; Luke 6:20-49

When Jesus saw the multitudes following Him,
 He went to the top of a hill to teach
 His disciples and the multitudes.

Lord, thank You for blessing me:
    When I am poor in spirit—totally dependent on You—
    The kingdom of Heaven is mine.
When I mourn—broken over sin in my life,
    You will give me consolation.
When I am meek—willing to set aside my rights—
    You will give me possession of the earth.
When I hunger and thirst after righteousness,
    Having a desire for outward holiness,
    I will be satisfied by Your presence.
When I am merciful—looking on others,
    Mercy will be shown to me.
When I am pure—a desire for inward holiness—
    Then I shall see You.
When I am a peacemaker—building
    Relationship in others,
    I will be called a child of God.
When I am persecuted for righteousness' sake—
    Suffering for You,
    Mine will be the kingdom of Heaven.
When I am persecuted falsely—because of
    My loyalty to the person of Christ,
    I will accept it as a rich reward
Because this is what the enemies of God
    Did to the prophets and to Jesus Christ.

Lord, I want to be like the salt of the earth
    So I can make people thirsty for Jesus.
If I lose my ability to influence people,
    I might as well be thrown away
    Like salt that has lost its saltiness.
I want to be a light to the world
    So people will know how to
    Find their way to Jesus.

People don't put a candle under a bucket,
>They put it in a candle-holder
>So it can light a whole room.

I want to shine before You so
>*People can see my good works*
>*And glorify You, the heavenly Father.*

Lord, I know Jesus didn't come to do away with
>The teachings of the Old Testament
>But to fulfill the prophecies about Him.
I know not one dot and comma can be changed
>In the Old Testament Scriptures;
Everything it promised will come to pass,
>Just the way it was predicted.
Any one who breaks one commandment of the Law,
>Or teaches people to break them,
>Will be last in the Kingdom.
When I keep or teach others to keep the commandments,
>I will be great in the Kingdom.
I accept Your imputed righteousness to me
>Which is greater than the self-righteousness
>Of the scribes and Pharisees.
I know You said whoever kills
>Will be in danger of eternal judgment,
May I never become so angry with anyone
>That I condemn them to hell
Because You said I would be in danger
>Of going to hell myself.
As I begin to pray and remember
>Someone who is mad at me,
I will stop praying and go reconcile
>Myself with that offended person,
>Then I will pray to You.

I will come to terms with those who sue me
    Before I meet them in court,
Lest the judge agree with my opponent
      And they put me in jail
      Or make me pay the full cost.

Lord, I know You said for us not to commit adultery,
    I won't even have impure intentions,
    Lest I commit adultery in my heart.
If anything entices me to sin,
    I will rid it from my life.
It's best for me to get rid of a stumbling block
    Than to lose my testimony or life.
If part of my body is a snare to me,
    I will ignore it, as though it's not there.
It's best to lose the use of part of my body
    Than to destroy the whole body
    And perhaps even the soul.

Jesus quoted the Old Testament that a notice of divorce
    Must be given before putting away a spouse.
Then Jesus said, "If you put away a wife for any reason,
    Other than unfaithfulness,
    Both you and she have become adulterers."
Jesus said, "You have been taught not to break an oath
    By the Old Testament standards."
But Jesus said don't even swear by anything
    Because you can't make one hair black or white.
Jesus commanded us to tell people what we will do,
    But, we should do what we say;
    Our word of promise should be enough.
Jesus quoted the ancients, "An eye for an eye
    And a tooth for a tooth"
    But that principle is not our standard.

Jesus also said don't take revenge;
  If someone hits you on the right cheek,
  Offer them the left cheek.
If a man asks to take away your coat,
  Give him your overcoat also.
If anyone orders you to go one mile,
  Go two miles with him.
If anyone wants to borrow something,
  Do not turn that person down.

Lord, You said to love my enemies,
  I will do good to those who hate me.
You said to bless those who hate me;
  I will pray for those who despitefully use me,
  I will treat them as I want to be treated.
Jesus said, "If you love only those who love you,
  There is no spiritual reward in that,
  Even sinners love those who love them."
I will love my enemies
  And do good things to those who hate me,
Because You said, "I would receive a rich reward,
  And show everyone that I am a child of the Most High."

Lord, I will not practice my piety before people,
  To be "holy" in their eyes,
  Because You will not reward it.
I won't show off when I give money
  Because that would be hypocritical,
  Recognition is the only reward a hypocrite gets.
When I give my money secretly,
  I won't let my left hand know
  What my right hand is doing.
Lord, You know all intentions, and see all gifts,
  And will reward me if I give humbly and honestly.

Lord, I will not be like the hypocrites when I pray,
>   Because they love to pray before people to get attention
>   And that's all the reward they'll get.
I will go to my prayer closet
>   Where no one can see or hear me,
>   Then I'll pray to You, my Father, in secret.
Then you'll see my sincerity in private
>   And reward me openly.
I'll not rattle off long prayers like the unsaved,
>   Who think they'll be heard
>   Because they pray a long time.
I realize You know everything in my heart,
>   You know my needs before I pray.

Lord, when I pray, I'll follow this pattern:
>   My Father in Heaven, may Your name be holy,
>   In my life on earth as Your name is holy in Heaven.
May Your Kingdom come in my life
>   On earth as Your Kingdom rules in Heaven.
May Your will be done in my life
>   On earth as Your will is done in Heaven.
Give me daily bread for this day
>   And forgive the consequences my sin,
>   As I forgive the sins of those who hurt me.
Do not let me be tempted to do evil
>   And protect me from the evil one,
For You have the ability to answer this prayer.
>   Let Your Kingdom rule my life,
>   May You get credit when these prayers are answered.

Lord, if I forgive the failings of others,
>   You will forgive my faults.
But if I refuse to forgive others
>   You will not forgive me.

Lord, I will not fast with an outward "religious" face,
     For that is just to get attention from others,
     The "attention" they get is their reward.
I will dress my normal way when I fast
     So no one will know I'm fasting.
My fast will be a secret between You and me
     And You will reward me with the answers I seek.

Lord, I'll not pile up wealth on earth
     Where inflation or corruption will destroy it.
I'll deposit my wealth in Your heavenly bank,
     Where nothing can destroy it.
Therefore, I will put my treasure
     Where I make a heart commitment.

Lord, may I see things clearly,
     Give me light and understanding in my heart
Because when my eye is clouded with lust and evil thoughts,
     My heart will be blinded by darkness;
     I'll not understand or seek spiritual things.
I'll not serve two masters—God and money,
     Because I'll naturally love one and reject the other.
So Lord, what must I do?
     I won't worry about clothes, entertainment or food.
My life is far more important than
     What I eat, or wear.
The birds will be my example, they don't worry,
     About sowing, reaping or eating food.

Lord, I'm more important to You than birds,
     I know worry will not give me anything I need.
I'll let the lilies of the field be my example for clothing
     They don't worry about their appearance.
Yet Solomon in all his glory
     Is not as beautiful as the lilies.

So Lord, since You wonderfully care for the flowers
    That are here today, and gone tomorrow,
    I know You can take care of me.
Lord, forgive me when I have so little faith,
    About the necessities of life.

Lord, I'll not worry about having enough food and clothing
    Because You know I need them;
    These are the things unsaved people worry about.
I'll seek first Your Kingdom and righteousness,
    Then all these things will be added to me.
I'll not be anxious about tomorrow
    Since You'll take care of tomorrow's needs;
    I'll live one day at a time.

Lord, I'll not criticize others, so they won't criticize me,
    Because the way I treat others
    Is the way they will treat me.
What I give to others is what they'll give me,
    So Lord make me a gracious giver.

Lord, I'll not criticize the small trash in another's eye,
    When my eye is full of garbage.
I can't say, "Let me clean out Your eye,"
    When my eye is full of dirt and filth.
I must first cleanse my eyes
    Before I can help anyone see more clearly.

Lord, I will not give beautiful pearls to pigs,
    They will stomp them into the mud
And then they will turn to attack me,
    So I'll not give "holy things" to evil people.

Lord, I will ask in prayer for the things You can do,
    For You give to those who ask.
I will seek for the things I need,

For You supply those who seek.
When a door is closed for the things I need,
    I will constantly knock
    For You will open and allow me to find.
I would never give anyone a stone
    When they need bread to eat.
I would never give anyone a snake
    When they ask for a fish to eat.
Since hard-hearted people give good things to their children
    Then I know that You the Heavenly Father will give
    Good gifts to Your children when they ask.

Lord, I will do good things for other people
    That I want them to do for me.

Lord, I will enter Your presence by the narrow door
    Since the road to hell is wide and inviting,
    And most of the crowd takes this road.
But the door to Your presence is small
    And the path to eternal life is narrow.
    So only a few find it.

Lord, I will watch out for false preachers disguised as sheep,
    Because they are ravenous wolves
    Who will eat up young Christians.
I can tell people by their fruit
    Just as I can't pick good fruit from weeds,
    So false preachers are known by their evil deeds.
A good tree cannot grow bad fruit,
    And an evil tree can't grow good fruit.
A tree that produces bad fruit is cut down
    And thrown in the fire,
    That's what'll happen to false preachers.

Lord, those who cry publicly "Lord, Lord"
    Will not enter the kingdom of Heaven.
But those who do Your will
    Will be able to enter Your presence.
Others will cry out "Lord, Lord, I preached in Your name
    And cast out demons and did miracles."
Then You'll say to them, "I never knew you,
    Get out of my sight."

Lord, those who listen to this sermon and obey Your words,
    Will be like a sensible man
    Who builds his house on a rock foundation.
The rains came, floods swirled, and the wind
    Blew upon this house but it didn't fall,
    Because it was founded on a rock.
But those who hear this sermon and reject Your words,
    Are like a stupid man
    Who built his house on sand.
The rains came, floods rose and gale winds blew,
    And it collapsed with a mighty crash.

When Jesus finished this sermon,
    The people were amazed at its content
Because Jesus taught them with authority
    Not like the scribes and other religious preachers.

The Story of the Long Day

The long day is included in Scripture to show how busy Jesus was on this particular day in July, A.D. 27. It began at the breakfast table in Peter's house in Capernaum where Jesus taught, healed a demon-possessed boy, and explained the unpardonable sin. Then Jesus went outside by the lake to deliver an extremely long sermon. (This sermon by the sea is not printed in the action-events of the Long Day. It appears at the conclusion of the Long Day Scripture). Then Jesus sailed across the lake with the apostles where a storm threatened their lives, but Jesus calmed the storm. On the other side, Jesus cast 2,000 demons out of a man and they entered hogs, which rushed down a cliff and drowned in the sea. The owner of the hogs and the people insisted that Jesus leave. He returned to Capernaum that evening and healed a woman who touched the hem of His robe, then he raised Jairus' daughter from the dead.

The Long Day

Matthew 12:24–13:52; Mark 3:20–5:43; Luke 11:14-32

Jesus was eating breakfast at Peter's house,
>When a blind mute was brought to Him
>Who was also demon possessed.

Jesus cast out the demon so that
>The man both spoke and saw,

The crowd shouted with wild enthusiasm,
>"IS THIS MAN DAVID'S SON?"

But the Jewish leaders rejected the crowd saying;
>"This man cast out demons by the
>Power of Beelzebub, the ruler of demons."

Jesus knew their malicious thoughts and answered,
>"If satan casts out satan,
>He has an internal fight with himself."

Then Jesus continued, "When part of a kingdom fights
>Against itself, it will destroy itself."

Every city or house that fights against itself,
>Will collapse."

Jesus said, "If I cast out devils by Beelzebub,
>Then you and your sons can do the same thing."
>Jesus was suggesting they were sons of the devil.

Jesus then said, "If I cast out demons by the Spirit of God,
>Then the King of God's kingdom is here.

"You can't steal the things of a strong man's house,
  Unless you first tie up the strong man.
"Those who do not follow Me and My principles
  Are against Me.
"Every sin and blasphemy you commit will be forgiven
  But when you blaspheme the work of the Holy Spirit,
  You will not be forgiven because it's the Holy Spirit
  Who delivers salvation into your heart.
"Those who speak against Christ will be forgiven,
  Those who reject the Holy Spirit and speak against Him
  Shall not be forgiven in this world or the next."
Jesus told the religious leaders, "You are snakes, how can you
  Speak good things when your hearts are evil?
  You speak what's in your heart.
"Good people out of their good heart do good things;
  Evil men out of their evil heart do evil things.
"Every word you say—including casual words—will be
  Used to judge you in the final judgment.
"By your words, you will enter eternal life,
  And by your words, you will be punished."

Lord, I believe every word You've spoken and I will welcome the Holy
  Spirit to come and work in my heart.

The religious leaders asked Jesus to do a miracle for them;
  He answered, "You are an evil and selfish generation that
  Seeks miracles.
"I will only give you the sign of Jonah the prophet who was
  Three days and three nights in the belly of the great fish;
  So, I'll be three days and three nights in the heart of the earth.
"The people of Nineveh will condemn you because they repented
  Because of the preaching of Jonah, but you haven't repented;
  Behold, one greater than Jonah is here.
"The queen of Ethiopia will condemn you because she believed

All she heard and saw about King Solomon;
> Behold, one greater than Solomon is here.

"When a demon is cast out of a person—as I did earlier—
> The demon wandered aimlessly looking for a place to live.

"If the life from which the demon is cast out is not filled
> With the presence of God, the demon will return
> And bring with him seven demons worse than him.

"Then the lost state of the cleansed person becomes more evil
> Than the first state. That's what will happen
> To this present evil generation."

Lord, transform me, give me a new heart so I'll always do your will.
> *May everything that comes out of my heart bring praise to You.*

Then Mary, the mother of Jesus, came to the edge of the crowd
> And called for Jesus;
> Someone told Jesus, "Your mother and brother are calling for you."

Jesus answered, "Who is my mother and brother but those who
> Follow Me and obey My teaching." Then Jesus stretched His
> hands to His disciples, "Behold my mother and brethren. They
> who do The will of God are My family."

Jesus went out of the house and sat by the Sea of Galilee;
> A great crowd followed Him and overwhelmed Him;
> He got into a boat—pushed out a little from the beach—
> And taught the multitude.

> *Lord, I count it a privilege to be a member of your family. May I be worthy of this great honor.*

The sermon by the seaside was preached at this time. It appears at the end of the long day, so the reader can follow the events of this day.

Jesus Calms the Storm

Matthew 8:23-27; Mark 4:35-41; Luke 8:22-25

Just after noon Jesus said to the disciples,
> "Cross over to the other side of the lake";
> So Jesus dismissed the crowd.
The small boat in which He taught began sailing across the sea,
> And because Jesus was tired, He went to sleep.
A violent storm arose and waves broke into the boat,
> Almost swamping the boat.
The disciples woke up Jesus and said, "Master,
> Get up quick, we're about to drown."
Then Jesus rebuked the storm, "Be still" and
> There was a great calm.
Jesus asked His disciples, "Why were you scared?
> Don't you trust Me yet?"
The disciples were filled with awe and said,
> "Who really is Jesus that even a storm obeys Him?"

Lord, teach me to trust You
> *When the storms of this life beat on me.*

Jesus Heals a Violent Demon-Stricken Man

Matthew 8:28-34; Mark 5:1-20; Luke 8:26-37

After the storm they reached the other side of the lake;
> As Jesus got out of the boat He was met by a demon-possessed man.
The surrounding neighbors tried to chain the man,
> But he broke the chain because he was so powerful
> No one was able to control him.
At night he howled in the surrounding tombs

And cut himself with sharp stones.
When the demon-possessed man saw Jesus at a distance,
    He ran and fell at Jesus' feet,
Shouting at the top of his voice,
        "WHAT DO YOU WANT ME TO DO,
        SON OF THE MOST HIGH GOD?"
He cried, "DON'T TORTURE ME!"
    But Jesus said, "Demon, come out of the man."
Then Jesus asked the demon, "What is your name?"
    The demon answered "My name is Legion,
    For we are many."
The demon begged Jesus, "Don't send us away,
    Send us into those hogs."
There was a huge herd of hogs rooting
    In the field above the lake.
Jesus allowed them to enter the hogs
    And the whole herd of 2,000 hogs
    Stampeded into the lake and drowned.
The herdsmen ran to the neighboring towns
    To tell the people what happened to the hogs.
When the people came to investigate, they found the man
    Who had been demon possessed properly clothed,
    Perfectly sane, sitting at the feet of Jesus.
Then the people demanded that Jesus go away
    And leave them alone.
As Jesus got back in the boat, the healed man
    Begged Jesus to let him go with them.
Jesus said, "No…go home to tell your family and friends
    What wonderful things God has done for you."
The healed man visited ten towns in that area
    To relate the story of what Jesus did,
    And the people were simply amazed at his testimony.

The Woman and the 12-year-old Little Girl

Matthew 9:18-26; Mark 5:21-43; Luke 8:41-56

Jesus got back in the boat and returned across the sea to Capernaum,
    A great crowd surrounded Him when He disembarked.
Jairus, the leader of the synagogue, met him begging,
    "My little girl is desperately sick
    Come lay Your hands on her to heal her."
Jesus and the large crowd followed Jairus,
    People pressed on Jesus from all sides.
A woman who had been hemorrhaging blood
    For 12 years came behind Jesus in the crowd for healing.
She had seen many doctors, spending all her money
    And had not gotten better, but worse,
She kept saying in her heart, "If I can touch Jesus,
    I will be healed."
She barely touched the hem of His robe,
    When she felt that she was healed.
Jesus hadn't seen the woman, but He was aware
    That healing power flowed from Him.
So He turned to the crowd to ask,
    "Who touched Me?"
The disciples didn't understand what was happening,
    They said, "A large crowd is pressing on You,
    Yet You said, 'Who touched Me?'"
As Jesus looked around, the woman came forward
    Frightened and shaking, she fell at His feet
    And told Jesus the whole story.
Jesus said, "Daughter, your faith—not your touch—
    Has healed you."
While Jesus was speaking to the woman,
    A messenger arrived to tell Jairus,
    "Your daughter has just died."

But when Jesus heard the message, He said to Jairus,
    "Don't give up, just trust Me."
Then Jesus would not let anyone follow Him except
    Peter, James, and John.
When they arrived at Jairus' home, they confronted
    A commotion of professional mourners who were
    Weeping and wailing unrestrainedly.
Jesus announced to them, "Why this commotion?
    The little girl is not dead, she's asleep."
The mourners laughed at Jesus, so He went
    Into the house with only Peter, James, and John.
Taking the little girl by the hand, Jesus said,
    "Talitha, cumi" which is translated,
    "By the power of My Word, get up."
Immediately, the 12-year-old girl jumped to her feet,
    And walked about the room
    So Jesus said, "Give her something to eat."
Everyone was completely amazed,
    But Jesus said to them not to tell anyone.

Lord, give me faith like the woman You healed,
    Teach me to trust You for all things.

The Sermon by the Sea

Matthew 13:1-52; Mark 4:1-25; Luke 8:4-18

Jesus had taught in Peter's house early on the Long Day. He then left the house and sat in a boat near the seashore where He taught the multitudes. This sermon emphasizes the ministry that His disciples would do. It is included here after the Long Day rather than inserting it in its proper sequence in the day's action. This way the reader can see the sequence of events and how busy Jesus was on this Long Day which is symbolic of all His days.

Lord, be my teacher in all things,
   I want to learn from You.

Jesus left Peter's house to teach the multitude
   From a boat beside the shore of the Sea of Galilee.
"Look," Jesus said pointing to a farmer sowing seed
   In his field which was nearby.
Jesus said, "Some seed fell on the path next to the field;
   Birds quickly came to eat up the seeds."
Jesus noted next, "Other seed fell among the rocks
   And because there was little dirt,
   The grain sprang up fast,
But withered when the hot sun beat upon it,
   Because the roots had little nourishment."
Jesus continued, "Other seed fell among thorns
   And the thorns choked their growth."
Jesus told, "Still other seed fell on rich soil
   And produced a crop, some places a hundredfold,
   Some other places sixty, and some places thirty."
Finally Jesus said, "If you have ears to hear,
   Then you will understand the spiritual application of
   This parable."
The disciples asked, "Why do You use stories to teach?"
   Jesus replied, "Because you have the privilege
   Of understanding the secrets of the Kingdom,
   But the unbelievers don't understand spiritual truth."
Jesus continued, "When a person does something for Me,
   He will be given more till he has plenty."
"If a person does nothing for Me,
   What he has will be taken away."

Jesus quoted Isaiah to describe three who rejected Him,
   "They listen with their ears,
   But they don't understand what God says.

"They see with their eyes, but don't perceive
	Because their heart is hardened to God.
"So they hear the good news, but don't understand
		What God wants them to do,
		So they won't believe and become converted."

Jesus then interpreted the story for the disciples
		Because they had a believing heart
		To understand what the story meant.
"When a person hears the message of the Kingdom
		And does not respond, the devil comes to snatch the message,
		As the birds take the seed from the path.
"When a person receives the message but doesn't understand,
		He gives up when trouble or persecution comes;
		He is just like the grain sown in the rocks.
"When a person hears the message but gives up
		Because of worldly things or pursuit of money,
		It is like the seed sown among the thorns.
"But when someone hears and believes the message,
		He brings forth fruit: thirty, sixty, or a hundredfold,
		It is like seed sown on rich soil."

Lord, may my heart be good soil to receive and believe;
		Take away the thorns of sin, and the
		Stubbornness of unbelief.

Jesus then told another story of a farmer who
		Planted seed in his field.
"While he slept the enemy sowed weeds among the good seed;
		The workers told the owner what the enemy did.
"The workers asked, 'Do you want us to pull up
		All the weeds right now?'
"'No,' the farmer said, 'If you pull up the weeds,
		You'll also pull up the good grain.'

"'Let them both grow till harvest, then burn the weeds
But put the grain in the barn.'"

Lord, I know there are unsaved in our churches,
I will leave them alone and
Let You handle them at the judgment seat.

Jesus then told another story that His Kingdom
Was like a tiny mustard seed sown in a field.
While it is the smallest of things, it grows into the largest of trees,
And many birds rest in its branches.

Lord, I know Your message seems weak to the unsaved,
But it is the power of God to salvation
That will attract many to You.

Jesus then told a story that His Kingdom is like yeast,
When put in flour, the bread swells up very large.

Lord, I know when I humble myself
I become strong to accomplish much for You.

When Jesus continued to speak to the crowd with stories,
The disciples asked why He used parables.
Jesus told them He was fulfilling the prophecy of Israel,
"I will open my mouth with parables
To explain God's eternal mysteries."

Again, Jesus told a story that His Kingdom was
Like a treasure that was buried in a field.
Someone found the treasure, then went to sell
Everything to get money to buy the field.

Lord, I will sacrifice everything—including my life—
To obtain the treasure of eternal life.

Again, Jesus told the story of someone searching for pearls to buy;
>When he found the greatest pearl ever,
>He sold everything to buy it.

Lord, You are the pearl of infinite price,
>*I will give up everything to have You.*

Jesus told the final story of a big net
>That was thrown into the sea.
When it was full, the fisherman pulled it to shore;
>They put the good fish in a barrel
>But threw away the bad ones.

Lord, I know at the end of the age
>*You will separate the righteous from the evil ones*
>*Who will be thrown into the flames of hell.*
Those who are righteous will go to Heaven,
>*Because Jesus died for them.*

The Twelve Sent Two by Two

Matthew 9:35–11:1; Mark 6:6-13; Luke 9:1-9

Lord, send me where You want me to go,
>*I'll follow You anywhere You send me*
>*Just as the disciples followed You.*

Jesus went through the villages and cities of Galilee
>Preaching the Kingdom in their synagogues
>And healing all manner of sicknesses.
But Jesus was deeply moved when He saw the multitudes
>Because they didn't know where to turn,
>Like sheep without a shepherd.
Jesus said, "The harvest is extremely great,
>And there are not enough workers,

"So pray for the Lord of the harvest to recruit
More workers to work in the harvest fields."

Lord, I will work diligently in Your fields;
I will use my efforts to reach lost people.

Then Jesus sent the Twelve out with these instructions,
"Don't go to the Gentiles or Samaritans,
But only go to the lost people of Israel.
"As you go preach the Kingdom is here,
Heal the sick, raise the dead
Cure the lepers and cast out demons.
"Freely you have received your ministry from Me,
Now freely give it out to the people."

"Don't take any money in your wallets, nor a suitcase,
Nor a change of clothes or extra shoes;
Give as you have received, without charge.
"As you go, stay with someone who believes,
Give the home your blessings if it deserves it.
"If the people will not listen to you, or receive you,
Shake the dust off of that place from your shoes.
"God will be easier on Sodom and Gomorrah
Than on that place in the judgment."

Lord, help me be a courageous witness
In the face of opposition and persecution.

Jesus told them, "I am sending you as sheep among wolves,
Be as cunning as serpents,
And as harmless as doves.
"Be on your guard at all times, your enemies
Will take you to court or whip you.
"When you stand before religious leaders,
Testify what God has done for you.
"When you are arrested and stand before judges,

The Holy Spirit will tell you what to say
For the Spirit will speak through you.
"When they persecute you in one town,
Escape to the next place of ministry;
Your enemies will search for you everywhere.
"People reject Me and call Me 'the prince of evil';
What sort of name will they call you?
"The disciple is not superior to his teacher,
And the servant is not better than his master;
What they do to Me, they will do to you."
Jesus said, "Never be afraid of them who
Kill the body, but can't harm the soul.
"But be afraid of Him who can destroy
Both body and soul in hell."

Lord, I want to be Your servant to follow You;
I will accept what Your enemies do to me.

Jesus continued, "Two sparrows are sold for
A farthing, but not one falls to the ground
Without the heavenly Father knowing it."
"The Father even numbers the hairs on your head,

So Lord, I know I am valuable to You.

"Everyone who acknowledges Me before people,
I will acknowledge before My Father.
"Everyone who disowns Me before people,
I will deny before My Father.
"I did not come to bring millennial peace to earth,
But I have brought a sword of division.
"A son will be against his father, and a daughter
Will be against her mother.
"A believer's worst enemy may be right
In his own home.

"If anyone puts father or mother before Me,
    They are not worthy of Me.
"If anyone puts son or daughter before Me,
    They are not worthy of Me.
"If you do not take up your cross to follow Me,
    You are not worthy of Me.
"Anyone who prizes their life more than Me,
    They will lose it.
"Anyone who loses his life for My sake
    Will find eternal life.
"Those who welcome you, are welcoming Me;
    And those who welcome Me,
    Welcome the Father who sent Me.
"If you welcome the servants of God,
    You will get the same reward they get.
"If you give a cup of cold water in My name,
    You will not lose Your reward."

Chapter 10

JOHN THE BAPTIST

The Doubts of John the Baptist

Matthew 11:2-19; Luke 7:18-35

John the Baptist called two of his disciples to his prison cell
>Because Herod had arrested him for preaching;
>John sent them to ask Jesus a question.

"Are You the Messiah, or should we look for another?"
>John's disciples arrived as Jesus was healing the sick,
>Casting out evil spirits, and giving sight to the blind.

Then Jesus told the disciples, "Go tell John
>What you have seen and heard.

"The blind see, the lame walk, lepers are healed,
>The deaf hear, and the dead are raised.

"The good news of the Gospel is proclaimed,
>Happy is the man who doesn't lose faith in Me."

Lord, increase my faith; I want unquestioning allegiance.

When the disciples left to return to John the Baptist,
>Jesus asked the crowd,

"When you went to the desert to hear John,
>Did you see a reed shaken in the wind?

"No, you saw a prophet, but he was more than that,
>John was My forerunner, as predicted by God,
>'I will send My messenger before Messiah comes.'"

Then Jesus said, "There is not a man born

Of woman who is greater than John the Baptist,
And anyone who considers himself least in the Kingdom
Is greater than John the Baptist."

Lord, I want to be that person.

Jesus said, "Everyone—even tax-collectors—
Believed and were baptized by John,
But the Jewish leaders rejected God's plan
So they refused John's baptism."
Jesus asked, "What is this generation like?"
Then He answered, "You are like children
Complaining about the games they play.
"John the Baptist came first and didn't drink wine;
So you said, 'He is crazy.'
"Then I, the Son of Man, come enjoying food and drink,
And you call Me a glutton and drunkard.
"Make up your minds what you want;
You are a generation that rejects God,
You always justify what you think is right."

Lord, I accept Jesus for who He is;
Jesus is the Son of God, my Savior.

The Story of John the Baptist's Murder

On an early, cool spring evening, one week before Passover, the palace at Machaerus was brilliantly lit up like a torch on the hill. The people in the town below could smell the tempting aromas and hear the drunken laughter from the festive banquet. The meal was extensive; one course of food followed another. Wine and alcohol were abundant. Finally, Herod Antipas called for his thoroughly drunken guests to be entertained. Clapping his hands, he commanded the dancers to commence.

To the surprise of everyone, Salome, the alluring young daughter of Herodias, danced into the light of the room. Salome danced magnificently, tempting and taunting the men with provocative movements and gestures. Herodias recognized the burgeoning charms of her young daughter—her husband was clearly attracted to the young girl—so the mother coaxed her into this wretched, fleshly amusement to achieve her own ends. When Salome reached the end of her spectacle, the entire audience erupted into applause. Antipas jumped to his feet, wildly cheering. Then, with his guests as witnesses, he made a drunken vow to Salome: "You shall have anything you want, even half of my kingdom."

Salome smiled, her mother's words leaping out of her mouth like the fangs of a cobra. "Give me the head of John the Baptist here on a silver platter."

Silence fell across the drunken assembly. The shock of her request sobered men who previously in the evening had willingly given their sense of morality over to wine. Herod's countenance dropped. Anger gripped his heart, but having been put on the spot, he could not rescind his offer to Salome in front of his guests.

Antipas ordered his guards, "Go immediately and bring me the head of the Baptist."

The appointed executioner stepped out of the banquet hall into the cold spring night, walking up the steps from the palace to the prison. When he opened the rusty doors to enter with a torch, John the Baptist knew that his end was at hand. He knew he was to be sacrificed on the altar of Herod Antipas.

Within a few minutes, the guard came dashing down the stairs to the banquet hall, the silver platter in hand, the gory head of John the Baptist held high for all to see. The piercing eyes of the dead Baptist were open, accusing the man to whom the head was delivered. As the platter was offered up to Herod Antipas, John preached his final message: "REPENT."

Young Salome eagerly received the silver platter, then ran through the night to her mother Herodias, delivering to her the ghastly prize for which she had asked.

My Time To Pray

- Lord, if I have to die a martyr's death, help me to die like John the Baptist.

- Lord, help me to live as though each breath were my last.

The Murder of John the Baptist

Matthew 14:1-12; Mark 6:14-29; Luke 9:7-9

Lord, John the Baptist was the greatest man to ever live,
May I be as humble as he,
And fill me with the Spirit as You did Him.

Then Herod the Tetrarch said about the fame of Jesus,
"This is John the Baptist risen from the dead,"
For Herod had arrested John and chained him in prison
Because John had preached that it was against
Scripture for Herod to marry his brother's wife.
Herod wanted to execute John but was afraid
Because the people regarded John as a prophet.
His wife, Herodias, also wanted to kill John
Because he had embarrassed her,
But she couldn't arrange for it to happen.
During Herod's birthday, the daughter of Herodias
Danced before the guests at the party.
Herod was so delighted with her that he
Made an oath to give her anything she asked.
Her mother Herodias told her to ask for
The head of John the Baptist on a platter.
Herod sent immediately and beheaded John;
The head was brought in on a platter

And given to the girl who gave it to her mother.
John's disciple's came and took the body
    And buried it; then they told Jesus.

Lord, if I have to die a martyr's death,
    May I accept my martyrdom as did John.

Chapter 11

FEEDING HIS PEOPLE

The Story of Feeding the Five Thousand

Jesus was angered and heartbroken over the death of the prophet. The apostles encouraged Him to speak against this atrocity. The youngest apostle John agreed with Simon that this might be the catalyst that would stir the Jews to war. But Jesus did not want a confrontation with Herod Antipas. This was not the battle He came to fight.

The roads were filled with pilgrims on their way to Jerusalem for Passover. Wanting to avoid the crowds and any speculation about what He would do, Jesus got into a boat with His apostles and headed north.

When men and women on the highway along the lake saw Jesus leave, many abandoned their pilgrimage and began following Him along the shore. Jesus' boat landed near a large expanse of grass. He went to the top of a small hill to pray. But soon the multitudes gathered at the hill. When Jesus saw the people, as always His heart was moved. He began teaching them.

Because only men were required to attend Passover, many of their wives and children had stayed home. Jesus looked out to see thousands of strong men. If ever a dictator wanted an army to recruit and train for his purposes, this was the occasion. Jesus had only to proclaim Himself their leader.

Jesus ministered all day. The apostle Philip was the first to notice the shadows falling over the crowd.

Philip spoke to Jesus. "Lord, this is a deserted place, and the hour is late. Send the multitudes away, so they may buy food." Since Philip was in charge of food and provisions, Jesus asked him, "Where can we buy bread so that these people may eat?" Jesus was testing Philip; He already knew what He would do.

Philip had already counted the crowd. He knew there were about 5,000 men there, plus a few hundred women and children. Philip answered, "Why, eight months of wages wouldn't feed this many!"

Philip sent the apostles into the crowd to inventory what food was available. Only Andrew found food. Andrew said to Jesus, "There is a little boy here. He has five barley loaves and two small fish, but what are they among so many?"

Jesus said to Philip, "Make the people sit down, and bring the loaves and fish to Me."

The apostles followed Jesus' directions.

Jesus took the loaves, held them to Heaven and gave thanks: "Blessed are you, our God, who calls this bread to come forth from the earth."

He directed the Twelve to gather some baskets, then began breaking the loaves of bread, placing the morsels in a basket. He repeated the practice until the baskets were filled.

"Give this food to the people to eat," he said to Philip, who had watched the process. Then the apostles fanned out into the crowd. The baskets were never emptied, yet each person ate as much as he needed.

As the sun set, Jesus said to his apostles, "Gather up the fragments."

When the apostles had gathered up the fragments, there were 12 baskets left, one for each apostle—enough food for three or four days.

My Time To Pray

- Lord, I'm hungry today; feed me with Your presence.

- Lord, help me know that people are hungry who I meet in life, and help me feed them with Your Word.

- Lord, I pray for a great revival in the world, there are so many people who are hungry for something, and they don't know they are hungry for You.

Feeding the Five Thousand

Matthew 14:13-23; Mark 6:30-46; Luke 9:10-17; John 6:1-15

There was a great multitude following Jesus
    So He went up into a mountain near Tiberius.
The multitude followed Him because of His miracles
    And because He healed the sick.
They were on their way to Jerusalem to celebrate
    The springtime feast of Passover.
Jesus surveyed the multitude, then said to Philip,
    "Where can we buy food for them?"
Jesus knew He would feed them with a miracle;
    He was testing Philip's faith in Him.

Lord, may I be faithful when tested.

Philip answered, "If we had the wages of 200 servants
    There would only be a little bit for each one."
Andrew heard the conversation and found a young boy
    With five loaves of bread and two small fishes;
    Then Andrew said, "This isn't enough for all the crowd."
Jesus said, "Make the men sit down in groups of
    Fifty and 100 to make distribution easy";
    They sat on grass in the area.
Jesus looked to Heaven to bless the food,

Then He gave it to the disciples
And they distributed it to the multitude.
Everyone had as much as they could eat
Then Jesus said to His disciples,
"Gather the food that is left over";
So they gathered up 12 baskets full.
After the people saw the miracle, they said,
"This is the One who the prophet Jeremiah
Predicted was coming into the world to feed us bread."
The multitude rushed toward Jesus;
They wanted to make Him King.

Lord, feed me when I'm spiritually hungry
Just as You fed the 5,000 by the sea.

The Story of Jesus Walking on Water

By the estimation of anyone in Palestine—Roman or Jew—5,000 well-fed men was a potential army. Here were 5,000 men who wouldn't be distracted by hunger. Jesus could feed them miraculously. If they were wounded in battle, Jesus could heal them. Surely these men could be motivated to follow the Messiah in a campaign to liberate the Holy Land.

The same thoughts occurred to a number of the 5,000. The men were carried away with their potential and talked about making Jesus their king—by force if necessary.

Jesus directed the apostles toward the boat, then pointing across the sea, He instructed them, "Go to Capernaum."

Jesus walked swiftly through several clusters of excited men, then slipped between some high rocks into the hills. He needed to be alone, to pray and commune with the Father.

A desert storm rolled into the Sea of Galilee, and the hot air mixing with cool breezes off the cold water unleashed a torrential rain.

As Jesus was praying, He looked out and saw the disciples caught in the storm. If they tried to make it to shore, the boat would be pounded to pieces. If they stayed on the lake, the boat would capsize. Immediately, Jesus left His place of prayer and went to them—walking across the water.

The waves grew higher; even the apostles who were hardened fishermen were frightened.

"YE-E-E-A-A-A-I-I-I!" one of the apostles screamed when he saw Jesus. "It's a ghost!"The scream startled the other apostles, who caught sight of the apparition walking on the water. They stopped pulling on the oars and stared, dumbstruck.

Another one of them yelled again, "It's a ghost!"

Peter didn't believe it. He knew this was no spirit, but someone dear. The stout, red-bearded fisherman yelled, "It's the Lord!" Jesus called out, "It is I! Do not be afraid."

Ever impetuous, Peter shouted out over the water, "Lord...if it is You, tell me to come to You, and I will walk to You on the water."

This was the kind of faith Jesus had been waiting to see in His disciples. He said to Peter, "Come...."

Instinctively, Peter leaped from the boat. He began walking toward his Master on the water.

At first, the eyes of Peter were riveted on Jesus. In faith, the big fisherman was doing something no man had ever done. But when Peter saw the waves swirling around him, he became afraid and began to sink. Peter looked to Jesus with beseeching eyes. He cried out, "Lord, save me!"

Jesus stretched out a hand and caught him, asking, "O you of little faith, why did you doubt?"

When Jesus and Peter got into the boat, Jesus commanded the raging waves, "Peace...be still." And the wind ceased.

My Time To Pray

- Lord, thank You for coming to me in the past when I had storms in my life. I know You will come to help me in future storms.

- Lord, I know You send me into the storm, as You sent the disciples into the storm. Help me to learn Your purpose for storms in my life.

- Lord, I worship You for helping me through my storms, just as You delivered the disciples from their storms.

Jesus Walks on the Water

Matthew 14:24-33; Mark 6:47-51; John 6:15-21

Jesus sent His disciples across the sea
>In a boat to Capernaum.
He then went to an isolated area
>In the mountains to pray.
A storm broke over the sea and the disciples
>Were afraid because they couldn't
>Control the boat in the massive waves.
About 3 A.M. Jesus saw their distress
>And went to them, walking on the water.

Lord, when I am distressed because of problems,
>*Come to meet my needs and help me get through*
>*The problems of my life.*

The disciples were frightened when they saw Jesus
>Because they thought He was a ghost.
Jesus made as if He would pass them by,
>So they cried out to Him.

Jesus answered, "It is I, do not be afraid";
>> Then Peter yelled to Jesus,
"Lord, if this is You, let me
>> Come to You, walking on the water."
Jesus answered with one word, "Come!"
>> Peter jumped out of the boat
>> And walked on the water to Jesus.
But then he looked at the waves
>> And began to sink into the sea.
Peter yelled to Jesus, "Save me";
>> Jesus stretched out His hand to him
>> And lifted Peter up.
Jesus told Peter, "Why do you have such
>> Little faith? Why do you doubt Me?"

Lord, may I yell out a desperate prayer
>> *When an emergency threatens me?"*

When they got into the boat, the winds ceased
>> And they worshiped Jesus, saying,
>> "Truly, You are the Son of God."

Sermon on the Bread of Life

John 6:22-71

The next day the crowd walked around the sea toward Capernaum
>> And they only saw one boat there.
And they knew Jesus didn't get into the boat
>> With the disciples to cross the sea.
So they asked Him, "Rabbi, how did You get here?" Jesus didn't answer.
>> He said, "You seek Me because you saw the miracles;
>> Yesterday, you ate of the bread and fishes."
Jesus told them, "Don't work for food that perishes,

But work for the bread of eternal life
    Which the Son of Man offers you."
The crowd asked, "What must we do to perform
    The works of God which You do?"
Jesus answered, "The work of God is to believe
    On the Son whom the Father has sent."
The crowd answered, "Do a miracle for us
    So we can believe in You and follow You.
"Our fathers ate the manna in the wilderness that Moses
    Gave to them during the 40 years of wilderness wanderings."
Then Jesus said to them, "Verily, verily, I say to you,
    It was not Moses who gave you bread from Heaven.
My Father gives true bread out of Heaven;
    The bread of God is He who comes
    From Heaven to give life to the world."
The crowd said, "Please give us this bread";
    Jesus said, "I am the Bread of Life.
"He who comes to Me will never hunger;
    He who believes in Me will never thirst,
    But you don't believe in Me.
"All the Father gives Me shall come to Me,
    And I will not turn them away
"Because I come from Heaven to do the will
    Of the Father, and not My will.
"And this is the will of the Father that
    Everyone who believes in the Father will have eternal life
    And that I will raise Him up in the last day."

The Jewish leaders complained because Jesus said,
    "I am the Bread who comes from Heaven."
They argued, "Is not this Jesus the Son of Joseph;
    We know His father and mother,
    How can He say, 'I come from Heaven?'"
Jesus answered, "Don't complain! No one comes

To Me except the Father draw him,
>   And I will raise him up in the last day.
"It is written in Isaiah, 'All will be taught by God,
>   Everyone who believes what I say will come to Me.'
"No one has seen the Father except the One
>   Who comes to you from the Father;
>   He has seen the Father.
"The Jewish forefathers ate manna
>   In the wilderness, and they died.
"I am the Bread who comes from Heaven
>   That you may eat and not die.
"If you eat of this Bread, you will live forever
>   And the Bread I give you is Myself,
>   It is given for the world.
"Verily, verily, I say to you, the one who
>   Believes has eternal life;
>   I am the Bread of Life."

The Jewish leaders argued among themselves saying,
>   "How can this man give us Himself to eat?"
Jesus answered them, "Verily, verily, I say to you,
>   Except you eat the Son of Man, you will not have eternal life
"He who eats and drinks has eternal life
>   And I will raise Him up in the last day
"For I am meat to eat and water to drink,
>   And the one who eats Me will abide in Me
>   And I will abide in Him.
"I live because the living Father sent Me,
>   And the one who eats Me will live because of Me.
"This is the Bread who comes from Heaven,
>   It's not like the bread the forefathers ate and died;
>   He that eats this Bread will live forever."

When Jesus ended His sermon in Capernaum,

>Many of Jesus' disciples said this sermon

>Was too hard to believe.

But Jesus knew they were complaining, so He said,

>"If this sermon causes you problems,

What will you think when you see Me

>Ascending back to Heaven where I was previously?

"The words I spoke are Spirit and life;

>The Spirit will give you eternal life,

>The flesh cannot help you.

"Some of you have not put your faith in Me."

>Jesus knew from the beginning those

>Who believed in Him, and who would betray Him.

So Jesus said, "No one can come to Me

>Except the Father draw Him."

>Therefore, many disciples stopped following Jesus.

Then Jesus said to the Twelve,

>"Will you also stop following Me?"

Peter answered, "Who else can we follow?

>You have the words of eternal life;

>We believe and know You are the Messiah."

Jesus answered them, "I chose all 12 of you

>Yet one of you is a devil."

Jesus was referring to Judas Iscariot

>The one who would betray Him.

Lord, I will eat the Bread of Life

>*To satisfy my spiritual hunger.*

Questions About Ceremonial Cleansing

Matthew 15:1-20; Mark 7:1-23; John 7:1

Lord, teach me the right way to observe
Church traditions, just as You taught Your disciples.

Jewish leaders came from Jerusalem to Capernaum,
To find fault with Jesus' religious practices.
They were angry because Jesus' disciples ate bread
With defiled hands; they didn't wash
Their hands ceremonially before eating.
The leaders cleansed themselves ceremonially,
When they came from the market place,
They did the same to all eating utensils.
The leaders asked Jesus why His disciples
Didn't keep the tradition of the elders?
Jesus answered by quoting Isaiah, "This people
Honors Me in outward ways,
But their heart is far from Me."
"They vainly worship Me, teaching
Their doctrine as the Word of God."
Jesus told the Jewish leaders, "You leave
The Word of God and hold to your traditions.
"Moses told you to honor your father and mother;
The one who speaks evil of
Father and mother shall be put to death.
"But you say, 'My mother and father are
Better off because they gave birth to me.'
"This statement does not honor your parents,
You deny Scriptures by saying that."

Lord, may I be careful to always honor
My mother and father.

Jesus then spoke to the crowd, "A person
>Is not defiled by what goes in the mouth,
>But by what comes out of the heart.
"What goes into the mouth, enters the stomach,
>And finally is discharged from the body,
"But things that come out of the heart,
>Defile a person,
"For out of the heart come evil thoughts,
>Murders, adulteries, sexual perversions,
>Thefts, lying, pride, and anger.
"The things that come out of the heart defile a person,
>Not eating with unwashed hands."

Lord, forgive the sinful desires of my heart
>*And keep me from all outward transgression.*

Jesus Visits Lebanon

Matthew 15:21-28; Mark 7:24-30

Lord, give me faith to persevere in prayer
>*When it seems You are reluctant to answer*
>*As was the case of the Syria-Lebanon woman.*

Jesus left Galilee and went to Tyre and Sidon,
>And slipped quietly into a house for rest
>Where the crowd wouldn't exhaust Him.
But the crowds found out where He was,
>Then a Greek woman from Syria-Lebanon
>Came and fell down before Jesus.
Her daughter was possessed with a demon
>And she begged Jesus to cast the demon out.
Jesus said, "No one takes bread from the children,
>And gives it to the dogs under the table."

So, Jesus didn't respond in a positive way
But referred to her as a dog,
The Jewish word for Gentile.
But the woman showed faith by replying,
"Yes, Lord, but the dogs under the table
Get to eat the crumbs."
Jesus answered, "Woman you have great faith,
You will get what you asked";
And the daughter was healed.

Jesus Visits Caesarea Philippi

Mark 8:27–9:1; Matthew 16:18-28; Luke 9:18-27

Lord, instruct me how to love Your church
Just as You instructed Your disciples.

Next, Jesus went to the village of Caesarea Philippi,
And as they were walking, Jesus asked,
"Who do the people say that I am?"
The disciples answered, "Some say You are John the Baptist,
Others say You are Elijah, or Jeremiah
Or one of the prophets."
Jesus then asked, "But who do you say that I am?"
Simon Peter answered, "You are the Christ,
The Son of the Living God."
Jesus answered, "Simon Peter, son of Jonah, you are blessed,
You didn't think this up,
My Father in Heaven gave you this revelation.
"Peter, you have faith like a rock,
And I will build My church on
The solid rock statement of My deity that you spoke."
"The gates of hell cannot stop My followers
When they go preaching who I am."

Jesus then replied, "I will give you the keys
      To the kingdom of Heaven."
"Whatever you bound on earth will not enter Heaven,
      Whatever you lose on earth, will enter Heaven."
Jesus then instructed them not to tell anyone
      He was the Messiah, the anointed of God.

Then Jesus told His disciples that He
      Must go to Jerusalem to suffer
      Many things from the Chief Priest and the Scribes
And be killed by them, but He would
      Rise from the dead on the third day.
Peter rebuked Jesus saying, "This will never happen to You."
      Jesus turned and said to Peter,
      "Get behind Me, you are a stumbling block.
"You are not concerned with the things of God,
      But with the things of men."
Then Jesus said, "If any person will follow Me,
      Let him take up his cross daily and follow Me."

Lord, I don't want to save my life, then lose it;
      I will give my life for You
      And find Your purpose for my life.
What shall it profit me if I gain
      The whole world but lose my own soul?
      I will not sell my soul to satan.

Then Jesus added, "Whoever will be ashamed
      Of Me and My words,
I will be ashamed of them when
      I come into the glory of My Father.
"Some of you standing here will not taste death,
      Till they see Me coming in glory."

Lord, I will not be ashamed of You
  But will follow You to death.

The Story of the Transfiguration of Jesus

Jesus spoke privately to the three men closest to Him. "Peter, James, and John," He said, "come with Me." He pointed to the peak of Mount Hermon.

They climbed all that day toward the snowcapped summit; Jesus climbing ahead of the them.

As John and his fellow apostles crested a plateau in the side of the mountain, the breeze picked up speed, blowing a cloud rapidly toward the plateau, where Jesus now stood about 50 paces away. John saw there was something unusual about this cloud. Rather than absorbing light, sunbeams danced off the cloud.

The cloud settled over the plateau, covering them as a warm blanket. Peter, James, and John looked for their Master through the mist and then saw Jesus as they had never seen Him.

He appeared opalescent, as though reflecting the light from the sun. He glistened.

Through the mist, two men appeared to talk with Him. He conversed amiably with the men as though they were long-lost friends.

"That's...that's Elijah," sputtered Peter. "And the other one is Moses. I'm certain of it."

Peter felt a need to celebrate. He jumped to his feet, calling out to Jesus, "Lord, it is good for us to be here! If you wish, let us make three tabernacles. One for You, one for Moses and one for Elijah."

Suddenly, the shining cloud grew a hundred times brighter. A commanding voice spoke.

"This is my beloved Son, in whom I am well pleased. Listen to him!"

This was too much for the apostles. Terrified, they fell to the ground.

Then Jesus knelt beside them, saying, "Get up. Don't be afraid."

My Time To Pray

- Lord, I worship You now because of what I know of You in Scripture. I look forward to worshiping You in Heaven when You are glorified and transformed.

- Lord, teach me how to worship better than I now do.

The Transfiguration of Jesus

Mark 9:2-13; Matthew 17:1-13; Luke 9:28-36

Lord, help me see Your glory
And worship You as the disciples did.

Six days after Jesus spoke at Caesarea Philippi
     He took with Him Peter, James, and John
     And climbed up into the heights of Mount Hermon.
Jesus was transfigured before them,
     His face glistened as the sun,
     His clothes were sparkling white.
Then Moses and Elijah appeared
     And talked with Jesus
     About His coming death.
When Moses and Elijah departed from the Lord,
     Peter said to Jesus,
"Master, it is good for us to be here,
     Let's make three tents, one for You,

One for Moses, and one for Elijah."
While Peter was speaking, a cloud covered them
    And the three disciples were afraid.
Then a voice spoke from the cloud,
    "This is my beloved Son,
    In whom I am well pleased; hear Him."
The disciples fell to the ground in fear,
    Then Jesus touched them saying, "Don't be afraid."
Then as they were going down the mountain,
    Jesus said to them "Don't tell anyone about this,
    Until I am raised from the dead."
The disciples asked Jesus, "Why do the Scribes say
    Elijah must come before Messiah comes?"
Jesus answered, "It is true that Elijah
    Must come to restore all things.
"But I'm telling you that Elijah has already come
    But the Scribes didn't know it
    And unsaved people will do to him as they want.
"In the same way I, the Son of Man,
    Will suffer because of them."
The disciples understood that Jesus meant
    John the Baptist was Elijah.

The Disciples Can't Heal

Mark 9:14-29; Matthew 17:14-20; Luke 9:37-43

Lord, teach me what to do
    When my prayers are not answered.

The next day Jesus returned from the Mount of Transfiguration
    And saw a large crowd listening
    As they questioned the nine disciples.
When they saw Jesus, they ran and greeted Him

Jesus asked, "What are you discussing?"
A man spoke up, "I brought my epileptic son
    To Your disciples who is deaf and unable to speak,
    But they couldn't heal him.
"My son foams at the mouth, and falls
    In the fire or water.
"He has an evil spirit—a demon—
    And when You were coming, it
    Threw him to the ground and wounded him."
Jesus answered, "O faithless and evil generation,
    How long must I put up with your unbelief?"
Then Jesus challenged them, "If you believe,
    All things are possible to the one who believes."
The father cried out, "I believe,
    Help me overcome my unbelief."
Then Jesus rebuked the evil spirit,
    "You deaf and dumb spirit, come out of him."
The evil spirit cried out and came out of the boy,
    Who dropped to the ground as though he were dead.
Jesus raised His hand and the boy arose;
    Everyone was astonished.
When they entered a house, the disciples asked privately
    Why they couldn't cast the demon out.
Jesus answered, "This kind comes out
    By continued fasting and prayer."

Paying the Temple Tax

Matthew 17:24-27

When they came to Capernaum, those who collected
    The temple tax asked Peter,
    "Why doesn't your Master pay the half-sheckle tax?"

Jesus asked Simon, "Do the kings receive taxes
     From his son or from citizens?"
     Peter answered, "From citizens."
Since Jesus is the Son of the Father in Heaven,
     And the temple belongs to His Father,
     Jesus doesn't need to pay temple taxes.
Then Jesus explained to Peter, "Lest
     We become a stumbling block to them,
Go to the sea, cast a hook, and
     Take a coin out of the mouth of
     The first fish you catch.
"Take that coin and pay the temple tax
     So they are not offended."

Lord, teach me how not to offend people
     So I can reach them with salvation.

Childlike Faith

Matthew 18:1-5; Mark 9:33-37; Luke 9:46-48

Lord, give me childlike faith
     To believe every word You've said.

As Jesus and the disciples were in Peter's house
     In Capernaum, Jesus asked them,
"What were you talking about as you
     Were walking here?"
The disciples didn't say anything because
     They were embarrassed.
They had been arguing which of them
     Was the greatest.
Jesus sat down and said, "If any would
     Be first, he must become last."

171

Jesus called a little child and set him
    In the middle of the disciples, and said,
"Verily I say to you, except you become as little children,
    You will not enter the kingdom of Heaven."
Jesus took the little child in His arms, and said,
    "Those who receive such little children
    In my name, receive Me."
"And those who receive Me, do not just receive Me,
    But they receive the Father who sent Me."

Lord, I'm like a child, not very smart
    And not very talented to serve You;
    I trust You as a child trusts his father.

Mistaken Zeal of John the Apostle

Matthew 18:6-14; Mark 9:38-50; Luke 9:49-50

Lord, help me be tolerant of believers
    Who are not members of my church,
    Just as You taught John to be tolerant.

John said to Jesus, "We saw a person
    Casting out demons in Your name
And we forbid him because
    He didn't follow You."
Jesus said, "Don't forbid him, one cannot do mighty works
    In My name or speak evil of me and be against Me;
    He who is not against us, is for us.
"Those who give you a cup of water because
    You serve Me, will be rewarded."
Then returning to the children, Jesus said,
    "Whoever causes one of these little ones to stumble
    A great mill stone should be hung

About his neck and be cast into the sea.
"There will be many who cause children to stumble,
But woe to the one who does it."

A Sinful Woman Anoints Jesus' Feet

Luke 7:36-50

Lord, may I worship You with my tears
    And the sacrifice of things precious to me,
    Just as the sinful woman worshiped You.

A Pharisee invited Jesus to eat in his house,
    So Jesus entered the home and sat down to eat.
A sinful woman heard that Jesus was there,
    So she came and stood behind Him crying.
When her tears wet the feet of Jesus,
    She dried them with the hair of her head,
And kissed His feet, then anointed them
    With the cruse of alabaster oil she brought.

Lord, may I love You so much
    That I worship You with the perfume of my praise.

The Pharisee was incensed and thought, "If Jesus
    Were a prophet, He would know the kind
    Of woman that touched Him, and kissed His feet."
Jesus knew the Pharisees' thought, and said,
    "Simon, listen to this story;
A certain leader had two debtors, one owed him
    $500, the other owed him $50.
"Because they didn't have anything to pay him,
    The leader forgave both debts."
Then Jesus asked, "Which will love him the most?"

Lord, thank You for forgiving all my sin-debts.

Simon answered, "The one who was forgiven the most."
      Jesus replied, "You are right."
Turning to the woman, Jesus said, "See this woman?
      You did not wash My feet,
      But this woman has washed them with her tears.
"You did not give Me a towel to dry my feet,
      But this woman has dried them with her hair.
"You did not give me a kiss of common hospitality,
      But she continued to kiss My feet.
"You did not anoint Me with oil as a courtesy,
      But she has anointed My feet with oil."
Again turning to the woman Jesus said, "Her sins,
      Which are many are forgiven her
      Because she loves much.
"Those who are forgiven little, love little;
      Those who are forgiven much, love much."
Then Jesus said to the woman, "Your sins are forgiven!"
      The Pharisees at the table inwardly criticized,
      "Who does Jesus think He is—God?"
      For only God can forgive sin.
Finally Jesus said to the woman, "Go in peace,
      Your faith has saved you."

Lord, I rest in the peace you've given
      Because I asked You to forgive my sins.

Giving Up Everything

Matthew 8:19-22; Luke 9:57-62

Lord, I will give up everything for You
      Because You ask for complete dedication.

As Jesus was traveling, a man told Him,
> "I will follow You wherever You go."

Jesus told him, "The foxes live in holes,
> And birds have a nest for their home,
> But the son of Man doesn't have a home."

Jesus said to another man, "Follow Me!" But the man said
> He had to go arrange for the burial of his aged father.

Jesus said, "Let the dead bury the dead
> But you go preach the Gospel of the Kingdom."

Another man said he would follow Jesus
> But he first had to arrange things
> At home before following Jesus.

Jesus said, "No man who puts his hand to the plough
> And looks back is fit for the kingdom of God."

Lord, I want to give You everything;
> *Forgive me for my ignorant lapses.*

Jesus and His Unbelieving Brothers

John 7:1-10

Lord, help me know when to take the advice
> *Of my unsaved relatives.*

Jesus' unsaved brothers counseled Him to go
> To the Feast of Tabernacles at Jerusalem.

They said, "Go do miracles so the multitude
> Will believe You and follow You.

"A person who wants to be known
> Doesn't do things in secret,
> But he manifests himself to the world."

Jesus told them, "The hour for me to manifest
> Myself is not here yet.

"The world does not hate you, but it hates Me
  Because I tell them their works are evil.
"It's not time for Me to manifest Myself";
  So He didn't do what they suggested.
After Jesus' brethren went to the feast in Jerusalem
  Jesus privately went on an out-of-the-way road,
  Arriving in the middle of the week.

Jesus at the Feast of Tabernacles

John 7:11-52

Lord, protect me when I'm in danger
  As You protected Jesus from danger at Jerusalem.

The Jewish leaders were looking everywhere
  Saying, "Where is Jesus?"
The crowd was confused, some said,
  "Jesus was a good man,"
  Others said, "He leads the multitude astray."
Yet no one supported Jesus publicly
  Because they were afraid of the Jewish leaders.
Jesus went into the temple on Wednesday and taught,
  Everyone marveled at His knowledge
  Because Jesus hadn't graduated from the best schools.
Jesus answered, "I don't think up the things I teach,
  This doctrine comes from my heavenly Father."
"If anyone is yielded to do the Father's will,
  He shall understand this doctrine
  Whether this is my idea or the Father's.
"He who does his own will, also seeks his own glory
  But he who seeks to glorify the Father
  There is no unrighteousness in Him.

"Moses gave you the Law, but none of you keep it;
 None of you are righteous before God."

Jesus said, "Why do you want to kill Me?"
 The Jewish leaders said, "You have a demon
 Because You think someone is trying to kill You."
Jesus said, "I healed a lame man on the Sabbath
 Eighteen months ago, and you hate me for it."
"Moses gave you the Law to circumcise a boy
 And you circumcise on the Sabbath."
"Yet you are angry with Me because I healed
 On the Sabbath day,
 Aren't healing and circumcision both a work of God?"
"Let's judge according to God's perfect judgment,
 Did we not both do right on the Sabbath?"

The crowd began talking among themselves,
 "Isn't this the man the leaders want to kill
 Yet they say nothing when He speaks openly?"
"Maybe they think He is our Messianic Deliverer
 So they don't do anything to Him."
Jesus preached loudly to the crowd, "You think you know Me,
 And you think you know where I come from,
But you don't really know Me;
 The Father who sent Me, knows Me
 And I know Him, because I come from Him."
The crowd wanted to take Jesus to the Jewish leaders
 But no one laid a hand on Him
 Because His hour was not come.
Yet, many in the crowd believed on Jesus
 Saying, "Messiah won't do more miracles
 Than this Man has done."
When the Jewish leaders heard Jesus was preaching
 To the multitude, they sent officers to arrest Him.

Jesus responded, "I will be with you for only a little while,
    Then I'll go to the One who sent Me."
"You will look for Me, but not find Me
    Because I'm going where You can't come."
The crowd talked among themselves asking,
    "Where is He going that we can't find Him,
Is He going to the Jews in the dispersion
    Or is He going to teach Gentiles?"

On Sunday, the last day of the Feast of Tabernacles
    When thousands of priests were parading with
    Pots of water to pour out as a drink offering to God,
Jesus shouted to the crowd, "If anyone is thirsty,
    Come to Me for satisfaction."
"He that believes on Me, will have living water
    Flowing out of his inner being."
Jesus was referring to the indwelling Holy Spirit
    But the Holy Spirit had not yet been given
    Because Jesus had not yet gone to glory.
Someone who had been in the crowd, said, "Jesus is a true prophet!"
    Others said, "He is the Messiah!"
But the crowd argued, "The Messiah doesn't come
    From Gentiles, but from Bethlehem,
    The village where David was born."
The crowd was divided because of Jesus,
    And no one laid a hand on Him.
The Jewish leaders asked the officers
    Why they didn't arrest Jesus;
    They answered, "No one speaks like Him."
Some said, "This man is not the Messiah;
    We know this man comes from Nazareth,
    We don't know where Messiah comes from."
The leaders rebuked them, "Are you also
    Deceived by this Man?

Have any of our leaders believed Him?"
Nicodemus (by this time a believer) said to them,
      "Does our Law judge a man before we hear Him?"
The leaders ridiculed Nicodemus, "Search the
      Record, no prophet comes out of Galilee."

Lord, thank You that I understand spiritual truth,
      And I'm not spiritually blind like the Jewish leaders.

Chapter 12

THE ABSOLUTE LOVE OF JESUS

The Story of the Woman Taken in Adultery

On the Monday after the Feast of Tabernacles, the fields around Jerusalem were littered with branches and leaves from the discarded booths where people had slept. Before the sun came up, Jesus was in the temple to worship, but even at daybreak the people were drawn to Him. A few hundred gathered around Him as He sat to teach. The Pharisees and priests remained at a distance, with a conspiratorial air.

Then a woman's cry was heard outside the gates.

"No! No!" The protests and shouts grew louder until two Pharisees appeared, dragging a disheveled woman. A pack of scribes and Sadducees followed, barking, *"Guilty! Guilty!"* The woman's eyes were wide with panic. She was thrown onto the pavement in front of Jesus.

One of the Pharisees announced smugly to Jesus, "This woman was caught in adultery. The Law of Moses commands that we stone her." He looked about him with a sneer. "But what do you say?"

The authorities were well aware of this woman's affair and had been waiting for just the right moment to serve her up to the healer from Nazareth. With a crowd of witnesses present, her sin would pose a prickly dilemma for Jesus.

"Everyone knows the Law," an elder Pharisee had reasoned. "If a man and woman lie together in adultery, they are to be stoned. If this Jesus is from God, He cannot deny God's Law."

"But Rome has taken away our authority to stone sinners," said another, "Only a Roman court can condemn a person to death."

"Precisely!" said another. "If Jesus says, 'Stone her,' He will be arrested for murder and inciting a riot. Then He will be Rome's problem. And if He says, 'Stone her,' where then is His Gospel of forgiveness?"

The woman wondered...the Pharisees wondered...the people wondered: What will Jesus say?

But Jesus said nothing. Instead, He bent to scribble in the dust with His finger.

The Pharisees began to grow uncomfortable. They demanded of Jesus, "Moses commanded that we stone adulterers. What is Your verdict?"

Jesus looked into the faces of the Pharisees. His quiet pronouncement was heard by all: "Let he among you who has never committed this type of sin, throw the first stone."

The silent crowd refused to move. Jesus stooped to continue writing.

After a few moments of embarrassment, the oldest Pharisee turned to leave. One by one, the Pharisees slipped away. Jesus stood to look around. Seeing none of the religious leaders, He said to the woman, "Where are the people who accuse you? Has no one condemned you?"

"No one, sir," she said. "They've all gone."

"Then neither do I condemn you," Jesus said. "Go and sin no more."

My Time To Pray

- Lord, keep me from being hypocritical like the religious leaders who only want to criticize.
- Lord, help me to show compassion to sinning people as You did to the woman.
- Lord, forgive any hidden sin.

The Woman Taken in Adultery

John 8:1-11

Jesus went early on the following morning
    And sat down in the middle
    Of the multitude to teach in the temple.
The religious leaders put a woman in the
    Middle of the crowd who was caught
    In the very act of adultery.
The leaders said to Jesus, "This woman was
    Caught in the very act of adultery,
The Law demands that she be stoned,
    But what do You say we do?"
The Jews used this occasion to try and trap Jesus
    So they would have an accusation against Him.
Jesus stooped to write with His finger in the ground,
    But the leaders continued to question Jesus.
Then Jesus stopped to say, "He who has not
    Committed this self-same sin,
    Let him cast the first stone."
Again Jesus stooped to write on the ground,
    Then the eldest leader left first,
    And eventually all the other leaders left.
Then Jesus said to the woman, "Where are those
    Who accuse you of sin?"
She answered, "They are not here to accuse me";
    Jesus said, "Neither do I accuse you,
    Go from here and sin no more."

Jesus Argues With the Religious Leaders

John 8:12-59

Lord, I need the light of Your guidance in my trouble,
There are always some who try to trip me up.

Jesus said, "I am the light of the world,
       Those following Me shall not walk in darkness,
       But shall have the light of life."
The religious leaders snarled, "You bear witness
       To Yourself, You are bragging and lying."
Jesus answered them, "My claim is true,
       I know where I come from,
       And I know where I am going.
"But you don't know anything about Me,
       You don't know the facts.
"I will not judge you now,
       But will do it in the future.
"The Law says to accept a statement
       If two agree about what happened
"Then I am one witness to My claims,
       And My Father is the other witness."
"Where is the Father?" they asked.
       Jesus answered, "If you knew who I am,
       You would have known the Father."

Later, Jesus was sitting where money was received
       But the officials didn't arrest Him
       Because His hour was not yet come.
Jesus said to the crowd, "I am going away,
       You will search and not find Me
       Because You can't come to where I'm going."
The Jews didn't understand, so they asked rhetorically:
       "Will He commit suicide?"

Then Jesus said to them, "I am from above,
     You are from this world
     And you shall die in your sins
     Unless you believe that I AM the Messiah."
The Jews asked again, "Who are You?"
     Jesus answered, "I AM the One I claim to be,
I could teach you much, but that would condemn you;
     I AM the One the Father sent to you,
     The One who sent Me is true."
But the Jews still didn't understand He was
     Telling them He came from God,
     And that He was the Son of God.

Then Jesus said, "When you have lifted up
     The Son of God, then you will realize
     I AM the Messiah from Heaven."
"The One who sent Me is with Me,
     He has not deserted Me;
"I do always the things that please
     The One who sent Me into the world."
Many people believed the words Jesus spoke,
     Then Jesus explained to them,
"If you abide in My words,
     Then You are truly My disciples,
"And You shall know the truth,
     And the truth will set you free."

Then the Jewish leaders answered, "We are Abraham's descendents,
     We have never been slaves to anyone;
     How can You make us free?"
Jesus answered, "Verily, verily, I say to you,
     Everyone who commits sin is a bond slave to sin.
"If the Son shall make you free,
     You shall be truly free."

"Yes, you are descendents of Abraham,
　　　　But some of you are trying to kill Me
　　　　Because My words have not set you free."
"I speak what My Father tells Me to say,
　　　　But you speak what your father tells you."
The Jews answered, "Our father is Abraham."
　　　　Jesus answered, "No, if Abraham were your father,
　　　　You would do what Abraham told you to do.
"Instead, you are planning on killing Me
　　　　Just because I told you the truth."
The Jews said, "We were not born out of wedlock,"
　　　　Suggesting Jesus didn't have a father.
The Jews bragged, "Our Father is God;
　　　　Jesus answered, "If God were your father,
　　　　You would love Me, because I come from the Father."
Then Jesus told them plainly, "Your father is the devil,
　　　　And you do the lustful sins of the devil."
"The devil is a murderer from the beginning,
　　　　And doesn't have any truth in him;
　　　　The devil is a liar, and doesn't speak the truth.
"I tell you the truth and you do not believe Me,
　　　　None of you can point out any sin
　　　　That I have ever done.
"If you were of God, you would listen to My words,
　　　　But you don't understand them
　　　　Because you are not of God."
The Jews accused Jesus of being a Samaritan
　　　　And being possessed with a demon.
Jesus answered, "I have not a demon
　　　　And I honor the heavenly Father.
"I have no desire to make Myself great,
　　　　The Father will do this for Me."
Then Jesus said, "Verily, verily I say to you,

If you will obey My words,
You will never taste death."
"Now we know you have a demon," the Jews answered,
"Even Abraham died, and You claim
If a man obeys Your words he shall never die."
The Jews asked, "Who do You think You are—God?"

Then Jesus answered them, "If I am just bragging,
It doesn't mean anything;
It is the Father who will glorify Me.
"But you do not know the heavenly Father,
If I said you knew the Father,
I'd be lying like you lie.
"Your father Abraham rejoiced to see My day,
He knew I would come into the world
And Abraham rejoiced in My day."
The Jewish leaders said, "You aren't even 50 years old,
And You said You've seen Abraham."
Jesus answered, "You're right, I existed
Before Abraham was even born,
I AM."
The Jewish leaders picked up stones to kill Him
But Jesus hid Himself and
Walked past them out of the temple.

The Story of the Man Born Blind

John 9:7-41

John was puzzled by the instructions that Jesus gave to the blind man.
Jesus told him to go wash in the pool of Siloam and he would see. The
pool of Bethesda was only a half a block away. Why hadn't Jesus sent the
blind man to wash in Bethesda? Across the street, a donkey drank from
a feed trough; it had water with which the blind man could wash the clay

from his eyes. But the pool of Siloam was all the way down the Tyropoeon Valley on the other end of Jerusalem. It was a long, tedious walk through many narrow arches, across shopping bazaars and down terraced steps.

The raggedly dressed blind man seemed to know the way to Siloam. He had not hesitated, but at Jesus' command had struggled to his feet, propping himself on a gnarled walking cane, and immediately set out for the pool as Jesus had instructed him. In fact, it was a trip the blind man had taken many times. *Tap...tap...tap...*, he instinctively began tapping his cane on the cobblestones, searching for a passage through the crowds. His steps were unsure on the uneven pavement, yet his feet had direction. He began walking toward Siloam.

Near the pool of Siloam, the steps narrowed and descended steeply. The flow of water emerged from Hezekiah's Tunnel and, with a friendly gurgle, emptied into a larger pool. Palms and a large eucalyptus shaded the gardenlike setting tucked away under the shadow of the outer wall of Jerusalem. The freshwater usually attracted a large crowd, most of who came to fill their water pots. But on the Sabbath, only a few moved about the pool enjoying a relatively cool autumn day. Slowly, step by step, the blind man descended.

Tap, tap, tap, the blind man stumbled toward the edge of the pool. *Tap...tap...SPLASH.* He found the water's edge. Dropping his walking stick to the ground, he bent over to lie flat on his belly at the pool's edge. Dipping his hands into the water, he splashed clear liquid into his muddied eyes. Then he splashed another handful of water into his face. Then he repeated the process again...and again.

Finally, he dried his eyes with the sleeve of his robe, then stopped suddenly, realizing he could see the fibers of his tunic. He jerked his head backward when he spotted his reflection in the water for the first time. He stared steadfastly at his face in the water, puzzled every time the waves of the pool distorted his vision. He lay on his stomach for a long time trying to match the image he saw in the pool with his previous self-perception.

"Aren't you the blind man that begs at the temple gate?" someone asked, surprised that a blind man's sight had been restored.

The healed man nodded vigorously. "I was blind, but now I see!"

"How were your eyes opened?" the stranger asked.

"A man called Jesus put clay on my eyes then He told me to wash in the pool of Siloam." He pointed to the waters of the pool. "When I washed, I could see!"

The blind man walked back to the temple where a group of religious leaders were gathered at the gate in heated debate about the morning's events involving Jesus of Nazareth. The once-blind man, waving his arms at the priests and Pharisees, shouted to get their attention. He told them of the miraculous healing. The eyes of the priests widened at the mention of Jesus' name. One of the Pharisees went to the healed man and callously pulled his eyelids apart to inspect his eyes.

"Where do you live?" the Pharisee asked.

"Get this man's parents," a priest demanded, and a young temple guard ran off on the errand.

The Pharisees asked how he had received his sight. He said, "Jesus put clay on my eyes, and I washed, and I see. It is a miracle from God!"

One of the Pharisees protested, "This man Jesus is not from God, because He does not keep the Sabbath."

But others had their doubts. "How then can a man who is a sinner perform such signs?"

One of the Pharisees confronted him, booming in rage, "I don't believe you were ever blind! You are a liar!"

"But...my parents will tell you I was born blind," the frustrated beggar pleaded, as a crowd began to gather, drawn by the dispute.

"You are one of the disciples of this rabble-rouser from Nazareth," the Pharisee accused him. "We will not allow anyone who follows Jesus to worship in the temple."

The healed man gazed once more upon the splendor of this place dedicated to praising the Lord, looking upward to the dome on the engineering marvel that towered a hundred feet above him. If he told these men he believed in Jesus, these things would be taken away from him. *I see this exquisite temple because of Jesus, he thought. How can I deny the One who gave me my sight?*

"Are you the parents of this man?" one of the Pharisees pointed to the healed man.

Both man and wife nodded, afraid to speak before the assembly of threatening faces.

"He claims to have been born blind," the Pharisee continued, "but clearly he is able to see. How is this possible?"

The mother's eyes were downcast in shame; she felt guilty for not running to embrace her son who had somehow been healed.

"We will deny you entrance to the temple," the Pharisee threw down the challenge, "If I do not get the truth, you will never return to this temple to make sacrifice to God."

Then turning to the parents, he snapped, "Is this your son?"

"Yes," they whimpered.

"Was he born blind?"

"Yes," the mother nodded more vigorously than the father.

"How then does he now see?"

"Speak up!" the Pharisee was shouting now. "How did he get his sight?"

"We know that this is our son," the father fumbled for the correct answer, a reply that would not incriminate them, "and that he was born blind. But how he now sees or who opened his eyes, we do not know." The father spoke clearly, "Ask him! He is of legal age. Let him speak for himself."

The healed man could contain himself no longer. He blurted out, "This is a miracle! Jesus is indeed a prophet."

"Jesus is a sinner," the Pharisee yelled at him. "Give glory to God."

"Whether Jesus is a sinner I do not know," the blind man answered, "but one thing I do know: I was blind, but now I see! "I already told you, but you wouldn't listen," he retorted in exasperation. "Why do you want to hear it again? Do you want to become His disciples, too?"

The crowd roared in laughter. This uneducated man was making fools of the religious scholars, his pragmatism confounding them.

"We are disciples of Moses!" the Pharisee proclaimed. He pulled his elegant robe around his bulging midsection, showing disdain for the simple man. "We know that God spoke to Moses, but as for this fellow Jesus, we don't even know where He comes from."

Jesus soon heard that the healed man had been barred from temple worship. He found the healed man talking to a crowd of people; he was still telling the story of going to the pool of Siloam.

Jesus smiled inwardly at the man's faith. Then He interrupted him to ask, "Do you believe in the Son of God?"

"Who is He, sir?" he asked. "Tell me so that I may believe in Him."

"I AM He." Jesus looked deep into the eyes He had healed. The eyes were no longer blinded, but were alive with love and faith.

"Lord, I believe," he said. He knelt and worshiped Jesus.

My Time To Pray

- Lord, thank You for giving me spiritual sight when I was blinded by sin.

- Lord, remove any spiritual blindness that remains from my unsaved days.

- Lord, You are the light of the world, guide me this day.

The Man Born Blind

John 9:1-41

Lord, take away my blindness and help me see
Your perfect will for my life.

As Jesus left the temple, He saw a blind man
    And His disciples asked, "Who sinned,
    His parents or this man that he was born blind?"
Jesus answered, "Neither did this man nor his parents,
    But to demonstrate the power of God."
"Each of us is given a task in life,
    We must do it in the daylight
    Because the night comes when work ends.
"While I'm still in this dark world,
    I am the light of the world."
Then Jesus spat on the ground to make clay
    And then rubbed it in the blind man's eyes
And told him, "Go wash in the Pool of Siloam";
    So he went and washed, and came back seeing.
The neighbors who knew he was blind were dumbfounded,
    "Is this the same one we knew who begged?"
    Others said, "It just looks just like him."
The healed man said, "I'm the one who was blind!"
    They said, "How were you healed?"
He answered, "A man named Jesus made clay and
    Rubbed it in my eyes and said, 'Go
    Wash in Siloam.' I did and now I see."
They asked, "Where is this Jesus fellow?"
    He answered, "I don't know!"
The crowd brought the healed man to the religious leaders;
    They also asked how he was healed.
The healed man answered, "Jesus put clay

On my eyes, and now I see."
The religious leaders criticized, "This Jesus
     Is not from God because He breaks the Sabbath."
But someone in the crowd answered, "How can a sinner
     Do such a great miracle?"
The religious leaders asked the healed man
     What he thought of Jesus;
     He answered, "Jesus is a prophet!"
The religious leaders said, "This man wasn't blind."
     So they asked his parents
     If the man was born blind.
The parents answered them, "We know that he is
     Our son, and that he was born blind,
"But we don't know what happened to him;
     Ask him, he is old enough to speak for himself."
The parents were afraid of the Jewish leaders
     Because anyone saying Jesus was the Messiah
     Would be excommunicated from the temple.
Then the Jewish leaders asked the man a second time,
     "Give glory to God, not to this Jesus fellow,
     We know He is a sinner."
The healed man said, "I don't know if Jesus is evil,
     All I know is that I was blind, now I see."
The religious leaders kept demanding,
     "How did Jesus heal you?"
The healed man became exasperated, "I told you once,
     Do you want to hear it again?
     Do you want to become Jesus' disciple?"
They cursed him, "You are His disciple
     But we are Moses' disciples."
The healed man was incredulous, "Why, here is a miracle
     And you don't realize Jesus opened my eyes."
"We know God does not hear the prayer of sinners,

But He hears those who worship Him and do His will."
"Since the world began, no one has opened the eyes
    Of a blind man. If this Jesus
    Is not of God, He could do nothing."
The religious leaders shouted, "You were born in sin
    Are you trying to teach us anything?"
    They excommunicated him also from the temple.

Lord, I will testify what You've done for Me
    Just as the healed man told what You did for him,
    No matter what the consequence.

Jesus heard they excommunicated him so He found him
    And asked, "Do you believe in the Son of God?"
The healed man answered, "Who is He?"
    Jesus answered, "You are looking at Him,
    I am the One who healed you."
The blind man said, "Lord, I believe";
    And then he worshiped Jesus.

I too worship Jesus because I was blind
    But now since my conversion I see.

Then Jesus announced to the crowd, "I come to judge
    So that those who think they see will become blind,
    And those who are blind will see."
The religious leaders asked, "Do you think we are blind?"
    Jesus answered, "If you were blind,
    You would want Me to heal you.
"But because you don't understand who I am,
    You are blinded to the truth of God."

The Good Shepherd

John 10:1-42

Lord, because You are my Shepherd, I will follow You
And trust You for everything.

Jesus said, "Verily, verily, those who don't follow Me
But climb over the wall into the sheepfold are thieves;
My sheep enter by the door because I am the
Shepherd of the sheep."

"Lord, I am Your sheep, I hear You call my name,
    And I follow You because I recognize Your voice.
"You go before me each day of my life,
    So I will follow You because I know You are good.
"I will not follow a stranger, but run from him
    Because the stranger does not have Your voice."
When Jesus used this extended metaphor,
    The crowd didn't understand what He meant.

So Jesus said, "Verily, verily, I am the door for the sheep,
    Those who come before are thieves and robbers
    But My sheep didn't obey their voice."
Jesus repeated Himself, "I am the Door,
    All who come by Me will be saved;
    They shall go in and out to find pasture.
"The thief comes to kill and destroy the sheep,
    I come to give sheep the fullness of life."

Jesus said, "I am the Good Shepherd
    Who will die for His sheep."
"A hired man will run away when the wolf attacks
    Because the sheep don't belong to him
    And he isn't their shepherd.

"The wolf attacks the sheep and scatters the flock;
    The hired man runs away because he is hired,
    He doesn't really care about the sheep."

Jesus said, "I am the Good Shepherd and know My sheep
    And my sheep know Me and follow Me.
"Just as the Father knows Me, and I know the Father,
    I know My sheep and will lay down My life for them."
"I have other sheep who are not in this fold,
    They are the Gentiles who will believe on Me;
    I will lead them also."
"These other sheep will listen to My voice
    And then all My sheep will be one flock
    And all will live in one sheepfold—Heaven."

Lord, I know You because I am Your sheep.

Jesus said, "The Father loves Me because I lay down My life,
    But I will take back My life.
"No one can take My life from Me; I willingly die
    And I have power to raise Myself from the dead,
    This is the assignment I was given by the Father."

The crowd was divided over what Jesus said,
    Some said, "He raves like a man possessed by a demon,
    Why should we listen to Him?"
Others said, "Can a demon-possessed man cause the blind to see;
    He doesn't sound like one possessed by a demon?"

When winter settled on Jerusalem, it was time for Hanukkah;
    Jesus returned to the temple near Solomon's Porch.
The crowd surrounded Him, asking, "How long will You
    Keep us in suspense? Tell us if You are Messiah."
Jesus answered, "I did tell you, but you didn't listen;
    I did miracles but you wouldn't believe them."
"You didn't believe because you are not sheep of My flock,

My sheep know My voice and obey Me;
    I know them and they know Me and follow Me.
"I give My sheep eternal life and they shall never perish,
    No one can snatch them from Me.
"My Father has given them to Me
    And He is more powerful than anything else,
    So no one can steal them from Me."

Then Jesus said, "I and the Father are One."
    The Jewish leaders picked up stones to kill Him.
Jesus responded, "The Father has directed Me to do many miracles,
    To help people who are hurting,
    For which one of these miracles do you stone Me?"
They answered, "Not for works of mercy, but for blasphemy;
    You are a mere man like us
    But You have said You are God."
Jesus quoted Scripture, "Your Law says men are gods,
    So if the Scripture is always right,
    Why did it call mere men gods?
"How can You say I blasphemed God when the
    Father who sent Me said I am the Son of God?"

"Even if you refuse to believe who I am,
    At least believe the miracles I do.
"Then you will realize the Father is in Me,
    And I am in the Father."

They tried to arrest Jesus but He walked away from them
    And crossed over the Jordan to stay near the place
    Where John the Baptist first baptized.
His disciples said, "John didn't do miracles, but everything
    He said about Jesus is true";
    So many people believed in Jesus.

Lord, I can be faithful without doing miracles
*   Like John the Baptist who didn't do miracles;*
I can pray for miracles and they will happen
*   Because I follow Jesus who did miracles.*

The Good Samaritan

Luke 10:25-37

Lord, may I love all people regardless of color or race,
*   Just because all are made in Your image*
*   And You love all the people of the world.*

A lawyer stood up to test Jesus with questions,
        Asking, "What must I do to inherit eternal life?"
Jesus responded, "You must love the Lord your God,
        With all your heart, soul, strength and might."
        Then Jesus added, "And love your neighbor as yourself."
Then Jesus concluded, "Do this, and you will live";
        But the lawyer tried to justify himself asking,
        "And who is my neighbor?"
Jesus answered with a parable, "A Jewish man
        Went down from Jerusalem to Jericho.
"He was attacked by bandits who beat him, and
        Stripped him of his clothes and money,
        And left him half dead in the road.
"A Jewish priest came down the road
        And passed by the wounded man.
"Next a temple assistant passed by on the other side of the road,
        Looked at the man and did nothing.
"When a despised Samaritan saw the man,
        He knelt beside him, cleansed the wounds with oil,
        And bandaged them up.
"Then the Samaritan put the man on his donkey,

Took him to an inn and took care of him.
"The next day the Samaritan gave the inn keeper
Money to take care of the man, and promised;
'If you need more, I'll pay next time I'm here.'"
Then Jesus asked the lawyer, "Which of these three was a neighbor
To the one who was attacked by the thieves?"
The lawyer answered, "The one who showed mercy."
Jesus said, "Yes, now go do the same thing."

Lord, make me sensitive to the needs of people,
Then give me initiative to do something about it.

Mary and Martha

Luke 10:38-42

Lord, may I know when to work with my hands
And when to sit at Your feet to learn from You.

When Jesus entered a village near Ephraim
Martha received Him into her house.
Her sister Mary sat at Jesus' feet
To listen to the things Jesus said.
But Martha was busy working in the kitchen,
So she told Jesus, "It's unfair for Mary
To listen to You, when I'm doing all the work."
Martha asked, "Tell her to help me in the kitchen"
But Jesus answered, "Martha, Martha,
You are upset over these trivial things.
"There is only one thing to be concerned with,
Mary has found the main thing
And it can't be taken from her."

Lord, may I always make Your main thing
My priority in life.

The Lord's Prayer

Luke 11:1-13

After a few days Jesus prayed all night and when He finished,
  The disciples asked, "Lord, teach us to pray!"
Jesus gave them the Lord's Prayer as their example,
As He had previously given it in the Sermon on the Mount.
He said, "When you pray say, 'Our Father, who is in Heaven,
  Holy be Your name
  Your Kingdom come
  Your will be done,
  In Heaven, as on earth.
  Give us day by day, our daily bread,
  And forgive us our sins, as we forgive everyone
  Who is indebted to us;
  And don't allow us to be overcome by temptation.'"
The Lord did not finish the prayer
  As He did on the previous occasion.
Jesus said, "What if you went to a neighbor's house
  In the middle of the night to borrow bread."
"You would yell to wake up your neighbor, saying,
  'A friend has just arrived for a visit,
  And I don't have any bread to eat.'
"Suppose your neighbor yelled back, 'I am in bed,
  My family is asleep, I can't help you.'"
Jesus said, "Though he won't do it as a friend,
  If the man kept asking and knocking,
  His neighbor would get up and give him bread,
  Just because of his persistence."
"So you can do the same with prayer, keep on asking,
  And you will receive.
"Keep on seeking, and you will find,
  Keep on knocking and the door will open.

"For everyone who keeps on asking—receives,
Everyone who keeps on seeking—finds,
Everyone who keeps on knocking—the door opens.
"If your son asks for bread,
Will you give him a stone—No!
"If he asks you for a fish,
Will you give him a serpent—No!
"If he asks for an egg,
Will you give him a scorpion—No!
"If fallen people like yourselves give good gifts to your children,
How much more will the Heavenly Father give you?"

Lord, give me faith to believe You for the things I need;
So teach me to pray.

Woe to the Pharisees

Luke 11:37-54

The Pharisees asked Jesus to eat with them,
So Jesus went to the table and sat down.
The Pharisees were angered because Jesus didn't practice
The ceremonial cleansing of the hands as they did.
Jesus, knowing their thoughts replied, "You Pharisees,
Wash the outside of the cup,
But the inside is full of evil and greed."
"You're foolish, God made both the inside and the outside
If you are righteous on the inside,
You'd be clean on the outside also.
"But woe to you Pharisees. You pay tithes on the
Mint that grows at your back doors,
But you forget about justice and the love of God.
"Woe to you Pharisees because you love the front seats,
And you demand people address you by a title.

"Woe to you Pharisees, because your hearts are like a grave;
People don't know there's death inside your body
So they walk by you, not smelling your death stench."

A lawyer asked, "Why are you reproaching them?"
Jesus said, "Woe to you lawyers, you strangle
People with religious demands
But you don't do what you require of others.
"Woe to you lawyers; you'd kill the prophets of God,
Just as your fathers did long ago.
"The Scriptures teach, 'God will send prophets and apostles
But you will kill and persecute them.'
"And this generation will kill God's servants,
Just as your fathers killed them in the past,
From the blood of Abel to the blood of Zechariah.
"Woe to you lawyers, you hide God's truth from the people,
You won't believe it yourself
And prevent others from believing it."

Lord, open my spiritual eyes.
I don't want to be blinded like these religious leaders.

Current Events in Jerusalem

Luke 13:1-9

Lord, help me see Your hand in the current events
That influence my life and service for You.

Some in the crowd told Jesus about the rebellious Galileans
Who Pilate executed and mixed their blood
With the sacrificial blood that was offered in the temple.
Jesus answered "Were these men the greatest sinners
Among all the Galileans because of their crimes?"
Then Jesus explained, "No, they were not!

All men are sinners, and all must repent
    Or they will likewise perish."
Then Jesus referred to the tower in Siloam that fell
    And killed 18 people. "Were they greater
    Sinners than these who live in Jerusalem?"
Again Jesus answered, "No, they were not!
    All men are sinners, so all must repent
    Or they will likewise perish."
Then Jesus told a parable, "A man planted a fig tree in his garden,
    Then came looking for fruit, but he found none."
The man said to his gardener, "I have been looking for figs on this
    Tree for three years, but haven't found any;
    Cut it down, why should it take up valuable space?"
The gardener answered, "Leave it alone for a year;
    I will dig around its roots and use fertilizer."
"If it bears figs next year, fine!" If not,
    Then we will cut it down."

Lord, in the same way You give people an opportunity to get saved;
    The Holy Spirit "digs" away at their hardened sin,
And He adds the nourishment of the Word of God and Christian Witness,
    But each person must eventually repent or
    Suffer the consequences.

Lord, I will pray for the salvation of my hardened friends.

Jesus Heals a Cripple on the Sabbath

Luke 13:10-17

Lord, help me keep my eyes on Your ministry to people,
    And help me overlook religious traditions that don't matter.

As Jesus was teaching in the synagogue on the Sabbath
    There was a severely crippled woman present who

Had been bent over double and for 18 years could not stand straight.
When Jesus saw her, He called out, "Woman you are healed!"
Then Jesus laid His hands on her and she immediately stood up
straight and began glorifying God.
The leader of the synagogue got mad because it was the Sabbath,
And said to the crowd, "There are six days for work,
And men ought to work during the work week.
"People ought to come get healing during the week,
But not on the Sabbath day."
The Lord answered, "You are a hypocrite! Everyone on the Sabbath
looses their ox from the stall and leads the animal to water.
"Ought not this Jewish woman who has been bound
For 18 years be loosed from her bondage on the Sabbath?"
The leader and his fellow Jewish officials were put to shame,
And the crowd shouted for joy.

Jesus Heals Again on the Sabbath

Matthew 22:1-14; Luke 14:1-24

Later Jesus went to the house of a religious leader for a meal;
There was a man there with greatly swollen arms and legs.
The leaders watched Jesus closely to see what He would do;
Jesus said to a lawyer, "Is it lawful to heal on the Sabbath?"
But the lawyer and the leaders refused to answer Jesus.
So Jesus took the man by the hand and healed him, then sent him away;
Then Jesus asked, "If your ox falls into a well on the Sabbath,
Will you not get him out immediately?"
The religious leaders had no answer for Jesus,
So He gave them parables to explain God's attitude
Toward needy people.
"When you are invited to a wedding banquet, don't sit
In the best seats, lest someone who is more important

Be given those seats and you are moved lower;
    You will be embarrassed because you must take a lower seat.
But when you go to the banquet, take the lower seat
    Then your host will see you and move you to a higher seat;
    As a result, you will be honored in front of the guests.
Those who try to honor themselves will be humbled,
    And those who humble themselves will be honored.

Jesus told a second parable of a man planning a banquet,
    "Don't invite your friends, relatives, or rich neighbors,
    Thinking they will invite you to their banquet.
"But invite the poor, the sick, and the disenfranchised
    And God will bless you because these people can't return the favor,
    And God will remember when He passes out rewards."

A Jewish leader thought Jesus had a good point, so he said,
    "I would consider it an honor to eat in the kingdom of God."
But Jesus answered him with a parable, "A man prepared
    A great banquet and sent out many invitations."
"When the banquet was ready, he sent a servant to get the guests,
    But everyone began making excuses; one man said
    He bought a field and had to go inspect it.
"Another man said he just bought a pair of oxen,
    And had to go try them out.
"Still a third man said he just got married,
    So he explained, 'I'm sure you'll understand.'
"The host was extremely angry and said to his servant,
    'Go quickly into the streets and back roads and invite
    The poor, the sick and the disenfranchised.'
"Even then there was more room, so the host said,
    'Go into the rural roads and look in the woods
    And urge as many as you can find to come to the banquet.'
"'I want my house full. None of those I first invited came,
    So they won't even taste the meal I prepared for them.'"

Lord, this is a picture of your invitation to Heaven. Many will
Reject Your invitation to enter Heaven and eat at Your table
But I will come and fellowship with You.

Count the Cost

Luke 14:25-35

Lord, I will follow You no matter how hard,
I will not turn back when the way is hard.

Lord, a great crowd was following Jesus, so He challenged them
To follow Him even though it is difficult and tiring.
"Those who follow Me must love Me more than he loves
His father, mother, sister or brothers, even his own life.
"Otherwise, You cannot be My disciples, but
You must pick up your own cross and follow Me.
"Don't begin following Me until you have counted the cost;
No one begins building a house but first determines the cost
Of materials and labor and if he has enough to complete the Project,
"Otherwise, when you lay the foundation, you find out
You don't have enough money to complete the project
Then you are embarrassed because you can't complete the house.
"Any general planning a battle will first determine if his
10,000 soldiers can win a battle against 20,000 soldiers.
"If a general doesn't plan well, he will have to send a team
To arrange conditions of peace or surrender.
"So living for me is a battle you must fight
Or you will give up and surrender to the world,
The flesh and the devil;
So you must renounce all that you have to be My disciple."

Lord, I renounce all.

Chapter 13

PARABLES OF LOST THINGS

Lost Sheep, Lost Coin, Lost Prodigal

Luke 15:1-32

Lord, the religious leaders were complaining about Jesus
     Because He received sinners, and ate with them.
Jesus answered them with a parable, "If you had 100 sheep,
     And one of them were lost, wouldn't you leave the 99
     And go search for the one lost sheep till you found it?
"When you found it, wouldn't you carry it home in your arms,
     And tell everyone to celebrate with you
     Because you found the one lost sheep?
"Even so, there will be more rejoicing in Heaven
     Over one sinner who repents, than over 99 self-righteous people
     Who think they don't need to repent."

Lord, I repent of my sins and come humbly to You.

Jesus told a second parable of a woman who had
     10 pieces of silver that was part of her marriage vow.
"If she loses one piece of silver, doesn't she search for it with a lamp
     And sweep the house till she finds it?
"Then she calls her friends to rejoice with her because she found it.
     There is joy by God in the presence of angels,
     Over one sinner who repents and turns to God."

Jesus told a third parable of a man who had two sons and
     The younger son demanded his portion of the inheritance,

So the father divided the inheritance between the two sons.
"The younger son took his money and went to a distant country,
    There he wasted his money on sinful and luxuriant living,
    Spending everything he had.
"When a famine came, the boy was hungry, so he took a job
    Feeding pigs. No one gave him anything to eat,
    And he decided to eat the pig's husks because he was starving.
"The young man came to his senses when he realized his father's
    Servants had more to eat than he had.
"He decided, 'I will go to my father and tell him I have
    Sinned against Heaven and against you. I am no longer
    Worthy of being called your son. Will you hire me as a servant?'
"The young man returned home to his father. While he was
    A great distance away, his father saw him coming;
    He loved him, ran to hug him, and kissed him.
"The son said, 'Father, I have sinned against Heaven and you,
    I am no longer worthy to be called your son!'
"But the father told the servants, 'Bring the family robe and put it on him,
    Put the signet ring on his finger, and shoes on his feet;
    Kill the fatted calf, let's have a feast.'
"'This my son was dead, but now he is alive;
    He was lost, but now is found,'
    And they began a family banquet celebration.
"The older son was working in the field. When he approached
    The house, he heard music, laughter and rejoicing;
    He found out from a servant they were celebrating
    His brother's return.
"The older son was angry and would not go into the banquet,
    So his father came out to invite him in.
"The older son said angrily, 'I have served you many years,
    I have never disobeyed you, yet you never killed
    A fatted calf for me or had a party for me.'
"'Yet, my younger brother squandered his inheritance in sinful living

And you throw him a big celebration.'
"The father said, 'You are always with me, and
    Everything I have is yours.'
"'It is right to celebrate because he is your brother,
    For he was dead, but now is alive;
    He was lost, but now he is found.'"

Lord, help me never leave You as did the younger son,
    Help me never be bitter over Your forgiveness of anyone;
    Help me rejoice with You over the salvation of all.

Three Stories

To the Disciples—the Unjust Manager

To the Pharisees—the Rich Man and Lazarus

To the Disciples—an Unprofitable Worker

Luke 16:1–17:10

Lord, help me be a good manager of all You've given me,
    And help me serve You with great integrity.

Jesus told the disciples a story of a rich man and
    His unjust manager who was stealing from him.
The rich man told his manager that he learned
    He had wasted his goods, and was fired,
    So the manager had to get the books in order.
The manager thought about where he would work next;
    He said, "I am not strong enough to dig,
    And I'm too ashamed to beg."
The manager then planned to adjust the books of those
    Who owed money to the rich man
    So they would take care of him.

The manager called the first, "How much do you owe?"
      He answered, "One hundred barrels of oil";
      The manager said, "Write on the debit 50 barrels."
The manager asked the second, "How much do you owe?"
      He answered, "One thousand bushels of wheat";
      The manager said, "Write on the debit 800 bushels."
The rich man commended the fired manager for such a shrewd act,
      Because the people of the world are more shrewd,
      In dishonesty than the people of the light.
Jesus said, "Shall I teach you to act that way—to buy
      Friendship dishonestly? No! If you are not honest
      In small things, you won't be honest in larger matters.
"If you have not been faithful in handling the money of others,
      You will not be entrusted with your own.
"And if you are unfaithful in handling worldly wealth,
      Who would trust you in the eternal wealth of Heaven?
"No one can serve two masters. Either you will love the first,
      And hate the second, or you will love the second and hate
      The first. You cannot serve God and money."

Lord, help me manage everything honestly that You've entrusted to me;
      Help me serve You with financial integrity.

The Pharisees who loved to make money laughed at Jesus
      When they heard the Lord's principles about finances.
Jesus answered, "You make people think you are honest,
      But God knows your greedy hearts.
"You pretend to be honest and humble before others,
      But you are despicable in God's sight.
"The law of Moses and the messages of the prophets have been
      Your guides in the former dispensation.
"Now the Good News preached by John the Baptist that
      The kingdom of God is ushering in a new dispensation
      Is now your guide.

"That doesn't mean the force of the law has changed,
>For it is easier for Heaven and earth to pass away
>Then for one dot of an 'i' of the law to change.
"That means the marriage law remains the same;
>Anyone who divorces and marries another commits adultery,
>Anyone who marries a divorced woman commits adultery."

Jesus then told of a rich man who wore expensive clothes
>And lived in great luxury every day.
"A poor man named Lazarus was lying in the street outside his gate,
>Covered with sores and the dogs came to lick them;
>He yearned to eat the leftovers from the rich man's table.
"The beggar died and the angels carried him to be with Abraham
>Where those who died in faith were located.
"The rich man also died, and was buried, but went to hell;
>As he was in torment, he saw Lazarus far off
>In the company of Abraham.
"The rich man shouted, 'Father Abraham, have pity on me;
>Send Lazarus to come dip his finger in water
>And cool my tongue, for I am tormented by these flames.'
"But Abraham said, 'Son, remember on earth you had everything,
>And Lazarus had nothing. Now he is comforted,
>And you are in pain.'
"'Besides, there is a great pit between us so that those
>Who want to come here from your side can't cross over,
>And those on this side can't come to you.'
"The rich man begged Abraham, 'Send Lazarus to my home on earth,
>To warn my five brothers so they don't come here.'
"Abraham answered, 'Your brothers have Moses and the prophets
>To warn them, let them listen to the Scriptures.'
"The rich man answered, 'That is not enough. If someone
>Were to rise from the dead and tell them,
>They would turn from their sins.'
"Then Abraham replied, 'If they will not listen to

Moses and the prophets, they will not repent,
    Even though one returns from the dead to tell them.'"

Then Jesus said to the disciples, "It is impossible
        To keep people from being tempted to sin
        But woe to those who tempt others to sin.
"He would be better off if a huge stone were tied
        Around his neck and he were thrown into the sea,
"Then he is facing punishment for tempting
        A little one to sin!
"Rebuke your brother when he sins,
        And forgive him when he repents;
"If he sins seven times in a day,
        You must forgive him each time he repents."

The disciples asked, "Lord, help us have more faith";
        The Lord answered, "If you had the smallest amount of faith,
        The size of a mustard seed, which is the smallest of seeds,
"Then you could say to a mulberry tree, 'Be uprooted
        And be cast into the sea,' and it would happen."
Jesus told His disciples another parable, "Suppose you were a servant
        Who plowed in the field or shepherded the sheep,
        Would you just return home, sit down and eat?
"No! First you prepare your master's meal and then
        Serve it to him before you eat your own meal.
"The servant does not deserve thanks,
        He does what he is supposed to do;
        Those who follow the Lord should have the same response.
"We do not consider ourselves worthy of praise,
        We have simply done what we were supposed to do."

The Story of Raising Lazarus

John 11:1-54

Flames crackled from the small fire. Jesus and the Twelve huddled around the flame for warmth. They had tarried in the cold highlands of the Moab hills for what seemed all winter, though they had been there but a few weeks.

"Someone is coming!" James the Less whispered. The apostles stood to meet the stranger.

Jesus immediately recognized him as the servant of Mary, Martha, and Lazarus, their brother. "Lazarus is sick." The servant spoke anxiously to Jesus. "Mary and Martha ask that you come immediately."

The Twelve glanced nervously at one another. The apostles knew and loved Lazarus and his sisters, but a return to Judea was ill advised. The people of Jerusalem had tried to stone Jesus the last time He was there. If the Jewish leaders caught wind of the fact that He was within their borders, they would likely try to arrest Him.

"This sickness will not end in death," Jesus told the servant. "Lazarus is sick for the glory of God,"

"What shall I tell Mary and Martha?" the servant inquired.

"Tell them that God's Son will be glorified through this."

During the next two days, Jesus did not mention Lazarus but explained to His apostles that soon it would be necessary for Him to go to Jerusalem. There He would suffer at the hands of the authorities, be crucified, and on the third day rise again. Even though Jesus constantly predicted His death, the apostles did not understand it.

After the two days had passed, Jesus awakened the Twelve early in the morning. "Get up," He urged. "We are going to Bethany."

Nearly every Jew experienced some level of holy excitement when approaching Jerusalem, but there was no excitement in the hearts of the

Twelve this day. As they drew near Bethany, one of the apostles instructed a boy to run ahead to Mary's house to tell them Jesus was coming.

Shortly, Martha came running and fell at Jesus' feet. Without greeting Him, she blurted out, "Oh, Lord! If only you had been here my brother would not have died."

Lazarus had already been dead four days.

Jesus, smiling, said, "Your brother will rise again."

Martha stood, trying to muster her strength, and said, "I know he shall rise again in the resurrection at the last day."

But Jesus had more immediate plans. "I am the resurrection and the life," he said to her. "Whoever lives and believes in Me will never die."

He placed His hands on her shoulders to ask, "Do you believe this?"

Martha answered him, saying, "I believe that you are the Christ...the Son of God, who was to come into the world." Jesus smiled and nodded, as Martha ran off to tell her sister. Soon Mary came hurrying down the path toward Jesus.

Mary said the same thing as her sister, "Lord, if you had been here my brother would not have died," Mary fell at Jesus' feet and began to weep.

Jesus, deeply moved by her grief, asked, "Where have you laid him?"

They walked into a narrow valley with limestone caves. Many of these caves had been fashioned into tombs. As Jesus approached the tomb of Lazarus, a crowd convened. As Jesus surveyed those gathered, he realized that no one there truly understood He held life in His hands.

Jesus wept.

Someone in the crowd saw His tears and said, "See how Jesus loved Lazarus!"

"Take away the stone," Jesus commanded, and four young men quickly rolled it away. Through the dark shadows, the corpse could be seen.

Then Jesus lifted His face to pray, "Father, I pray for the benefit of the people standing here, that they may believe you sent me."

Then with a loud voice, Jesus shouted: "LAZARUS...COME FORTH!"

The body wrapped in linen sat up. Quickly, several young men and apostles ran to Lazarus, unwrapping the cloths that had been wound about his body.

My Time To Pray

- Lord, help me understand Your patience when You delayed, or when You didn't come when Mary and Martha expected You.

- Lord, when my saved relatives die, help me look beyond the grave to the resurrection.

- Lord, thank You for eternal life now that I am saved and thank You for heavenly life beyond the grave.

The Raising of Lazarus

John 11:1-54

Lord, one day I'll die if You don't come back first,
I look forward to my bodily resurrection from the grave
Just as You raised Lazarus.

Jesus was sent a message from Mary and Martha
Telling Him that Lazarus was sick.
This is the same Mary that anointed Jesus with oil
And wiped His feet with the hair of her head.
The sisters reminded Jesus that He loved Lazarus;
Technically, Jesus loved all three of them.

When Jesus received the message He told His disciples,
    This sickness will not end in death
    But the Son of God will be glorified through it.
Jesus stayed where He was for two more days
    Then He told His disciples, "Let's go to Judea."
    They cautioned Him against making the trip because
    The Jews tried to stone Him the last time He was there.
Jesus replied, "There are 12 hours of daylight for walking
    So you won't stumble when there is light to see by."
Those who walk in darkness stumble because
    There is no light to guide them.

Jesus then said, "Our friend Lazarus sleeps, I go to awaken him";
    The disciples answered, "It's good if he sleeps."
They didn't understand what Jesus meant,
    So He said plainly, "Lazarus is dead."
"Now I'm glad I wasn't there when he died
    Because now you will believe completely in Me."
Then Thomas—the twin—said to the other disciples,
    "Let us go with Him, and die with Him."

When Jesus arrived, He found out Lazarus had been dead four days;
    Bethany was about two miles from Jerusalem,
    So many Jews had come to sympathize with Mary and Martha.
When Martha heard that Jesus had arrived,
    She went out to the graveyard to meet Him;
    Mary stayed in the house grieving.
Martha accused Jesus, "If You would have been here,
    My brother would not have died."
"But now I know that whatever You ask from God,
    He will give it to You."
Jesus told Martha, "Your brother will rise again."
    Martha said, "I know he'll arise in
    The resurrection at the last day."

Jesus said to her, "I am the resurrection and the life,
    And those who believe in Me will never die."
Martha answered, "Yes, I believe You are the Deliverer-Messiah,
    The Son of God Who was sent into the world."
Martha ran to whisper to Mary in a low voice,
    "The Master is here and wants to see you."
Mary immediately got up and went to Jesus;
    When the Jews who were mourning saw Mary leave,
    They followed her to the cemetery.
As soon as Mary saw Jesus, she threw herself at His feet
    Saying the same thing as her sister, "Lord,
    If You had been here my brother would not have died."
Jesus saw Mary's tears and the mourning Jews following her,
    He said with a deep sigh, "Where is the body?"
    Then Jesus wept.
The Jews responded, "Behold how much Jesus loved Lazarus";
    Other Jews said, "This man makes the blind see,
    Why couldn't He keep Lazarus from dying?"
Jesus sighed deeply. When He got to the tomb—a
    Cave—with a stone closing the opening
    He said, "Take away the stone."
Martha protested, "Lord, the body stinks
    He's been dead four days."
Jesus answered, "Have I not told you that if
    You will believe, you'll see the glory of God."
They rolled the stone away, then Jesus looked into Heaven,
    "Father, I thank You for hearing Me before
    I pray, so that the people here will believe in Me."
Then Jesus yelled with a strong voice, *"Lazarus come out!"*
    Lazarus came bound, hands and feet with swaths of cloth,
    And a cloth wrapped around his face.
Jesus cried, "Unwrap him and free him";
    Then some of the Jewish leaders saw it happen, and believed.

Results from Raising Lazarus

John 11:45-54

Lord, I know Jesus raised the dead, because
He gave me new life and new desires to worship You.

Therefore, many Jews believed in Jesus because
He raised Lazarus from the dead,
But others ran to tell the religious rulers what happened.
They gathered in council to decide what to do;
One said, "What can we do, this man does miracles?"
Another said, "If we don't do something, the Romans
Will come punish us and the nation because they will think
Jesus is fermenting a revolution."
Caiaphas the High Priest said "You're all dumb!
Let this man die instead of people;
Why should our whole nation perish?
"This prophecy that Jesus should die for everyone
Came from Caiaphas the High Priest,
When He was inspired by God to make this prediction."
So from that time on the religious leaders were convinced,
That it was right to plan the death of Jesus.

Jesus stopped preaching to the multitudes and went to the desert
And stayed on the border of Ephraim and Samaria.
People were journeying to Jerusalem for the Passover,
They were curious to see Jesus and kept asking,
"Do you think Jesus will come to this Passover?"
Meanwhile the religious leaders had announced that
Anyone seeing Jesus must report it to the authorities
So He could be arrested.

Lord, people hate Jesus because they love their sin
And they do not want to repent and follow Him.

Healing Ten Lepers

Luke 17:11-37

As Jesus was heading back toward Jerusalem, He
    Came to the boundary between Samaria and Galilee.
Ten lepers stood off at a distance as Jesus approached a village,
    They shouted out to Him, "Jesus, Master, have mercy on us."
Jesus answered "Go show yourself to the priest,
    Just as it is commanded in the Scripture."
As they obeyed Jesus and began the journey, they were healed;
    One came back shouting, "Glory to God for healing me,"
    He threw himself at Jesus' feet and thanked Him.
The healed man was a despised Samaritan;
    Jesus asked, "Did I not heal ten lepers?
    Where are the other nine?"
The only one who has come back to praise God
    Is this foreigner.
Then Jesus said to the man, "Stand up,
    And go home; your faith has healed you."

One day a religious leader asked Jesus, "When will the kingdom of God
    begin?" Jesus answered,
The kingdom of God won't come with outward signs,
    So you can't say it began here or there;
The kingdom of God stands among you";
    Jesus was referring to Himself as the King.

Lord, I don't just live for the day of the rapture
    Rather, I live today for You—Lord Jesus—the coming One.

Later Jesus talked about this with His disciples,
    "There is coming a time when you will look for Me
    To be with you, but I won't come to you physically."
"Some will proclaim I have returned either here or there,

Don't believe the report, nor go out looking for Me.
"Everyone will see Me when I return. It will be

As bright as lightning flashing across the heavens;

But first I must suffer grievously and be rejected.
"When I return the people will be just like those in Noah's days,

They ate, got drunk, married and ignored Noah's warning
"Right up to the day when Noah entered the ark,

Then the flood came to destroy them.
"My coming will be the same as it was in Lot's day,

They were eating, getting drunk, buying, and selling,

Planting and building right up till Lot left Sodom,
Then God rained fire and brimstone from Heaven

To destroy them all.
"The same will happen when the Son of Man is revealed

From Heaven to those on earth who reject Him."

"When the day of judgment comes, those on the house top

Must not go in the house for possessions,

Neither shall those in the field try to retrieve their things.
"Remember Lot's wife, anyone who holds on to the things of this life

Will lose his life and those who give up their life for Me,

They will save their life.
"At that hour, two will be sleeping in the bed,

One shall be taken, the other left behind.
"Two women will be grinding corn, one will be taken

The other one will be left behind."
The disciples asked, "What will happen to them?"

Jesus didn't fully answer them, but said,

"Wherever there are dead bodies, the buzzards gather."

Two Parables on Prayer

Luke 18:1-14

Lord, I know that prayer makes a difference in my life,
Forgive me for spending so little time praying.

Jesus used a parable to teach we should always pray and not give up.
There was a judge who was godless, and
Despised those who came before him for judgments.
A widow kept coming to the judge demanding justice
Against her enemy. The judge kept refusing her.
Finally he reasoned, "I don't fear God or people, but
This woman is pestering me to death with her
Continual begging for me to do something.
"I will give her justice because she continually asks for it."
Jesus said, "God will see that justice is done
To those who continually pray to Him,
Just as the widow got justice.
"Even when God seems to delay, He will answer persistent prayer,
And when I—the Messiah—return, will I find
People of faith on earth who continually pray?"

Then Jesus, gave the following parable to those who considered
Themselves righteous, but they hated others.
"Two men went into the temple to pray, one a self-righteous Pharisee,
And the other one was a sinner.
"The Pharisee boasted in his prayer that he was not a
Cheating, adulterous law breaker; but he fasted
Twice a week and gave a tithe to God of all he possessed.
"The cheating tax collector did not lift his eyes to Heaven,
But beat upon his chest to express
His sorrow for his sin; then prayed,
'God be merciful to me a sinner.'
Jesus said, "This sinful tax collector—not the Pharisee—was forgiven,

Those who exalt themselves will be humbled
And those who humble themselves will be exalted."

Jesus Teaches About Divorce

Matthew 19:1-12; Mark 10:1-12

Jesus left Galilee and came into the edge of Judea
    On the other side of the river Jordan;
    There He healed great multitudes that followed Him.
A Pharisee tempted Jesus, "Is it lawful for a man
    To divorce his wife for any cause?"
Jesus answered, "Have you not read what God said who made
    Them male and female; 'A man shall
    Leave his father and mother and cleave to his wife,
They shall be one flesh, so what God puts together
    No one should separate them.'"
The Pharisee asked "Why then did Moses say
    A man may divorce his wife by simply
    Giving her a writ of dismissal?"
Jesus answered, "Moses did it because of your hard
    And wicked heart. But that was not what God
    Originally intended for marriage.
"Anyone who divorces his wife and marries another,
    Except for fornication; commits adultery."
Jesus' disciple answered, "If that is the case then
    It is better not to marry!"
Jesus answered, "Some are born with the ability not to marry,
    Some are made eunuchs by others,
    And some became eunuchs for the kingdom of God."
Then people brought little children for Jesus to lay hands on them,
    And bless them, but the disciples turned them away.
Jesus said, "Let the children come to Me, and do not

Prevent them from coming to Me,
For of such is the kingdom of God,"
And Jesus put His hands on them and blessed them.

The Rich Young Ruler

Matthew 19:16–20:16; Mark 10:17-31; Luke 18:18-30

A rich young ruler asked, "Good Master, what must I do
    To get eternal life?" Jesus answered,
"Why are you calling Me good, only God is good,
    But if you wish eternal life, keep the commandments."
The young man answered, "Which should I keep?"
    Jesus said, "Do not kill, and do not commit adultery,
    Do not steal; do not bear false witness,
    Honor your father and mother
    And love your neighbor as yourself."
The young man said, "I have kept all these";
    Jesus said, "If you would be perfect,
    Go sell all you have and gave it to the poor,
    You will have treasure in Heaven, and then follow Me."
The young man was sad when he heard this,
    For he had great wealth.

Then Jesus told His disciples. "Verily, I say to you
    It is hard for a rich man to enter Heaven,
It is easier for a camel to go through a needle's eye
    Than a rich man to enter Heaven."
The amazed disciples said, "Who then can be saved?"
    Jesus answered, "No one from a human perspective,
    But all things are possible with God."
Then Peter added, "We have left all to follow You,
    What will be our reward?"
Jesus answered, "In the next world when I sit on My throne,

You—my disciples—will sit on twelve thrones,
>Ruling the twelve tribes of Israel.
"Everyone who has left housing, brothers, sisters, father,
>Mother, children or land for My sake,
>Will receive 100 times more when he receives eternal life.
"Those who are first will be last, and the last first."

Lord, I will be last in this life to be rewarded in Heaven.

The Selfish Ambition of James and John

Matthew 20:17-28; Mark 10:32-45; Luke 18:31-34

As Jesus was heading toward Jerusalem, He said to His disciples,
>"I will be betrayed to the religious leaders in Jerusalem,
>They will condemn Me and crucify Me,
>But on the third day I will rise again to life."
The mother of James and John came to Jesus with her sons
>And knelt in front of Jesus with a request.
"What do you want?" Jesus asked her;
>"Let my sons sit at Your left hand and right hand,
>When You come into Your Kingdom."
"You don't know what you're asking," Jesus answered;
>"Can they drink the cup of suffering that I'll drink?"
>The brothers answered, "Yes, we can."
Jesus answered, "Very well, you will suffer with Me.
>But as for the seats on my left and right,
>They are not for Me to give out;
>My Father in Heaven will assign them."
When the other ten heard about the request,
>They were angry at the two brothers.
Jesus called them together and said, "Earthly rulers have
>Authority over those they lead.
"However, this is not the way I do things;

If you want to be great, you must serve others,
> If you want to be first, you must be a slave.
"The Son of Man did not come to be served, but to serve,
> And give His life as a ransom for many."

Jesus Heals Blind Bartimaeus

Matthew 20:29-34; Mark 10:46-52; Luke 18:35-43

A large crowd followed Jesus to the gate of the city Jericho,
> Two blind men were sitting there
> One man was Bartimaeus, a blind beggar.
When they heard Jesus was passing by they shouted,
> "Have pity on us, Son of David."
The crowd scolded them, telling them, "Keep quiet";
> But they shouted even louder,
> "HAVE PITY ON US, SON OF DAVID."
Jesus stopped and called for them, asking,
> "What do you want Me to do for you?"
> They answered, "Give us our sight."
Jesus said, "Receive your sight, your faith has healed you";
> Immediately, they saw. They glorified God and followed Jesus,
> All the people praised God.

Lord, give me spiritual sight so I can see Kingdom things,
> *Help me to praise You in all I do.*

Zacchaeus

Luke 19:1-28

As Jesus was walking through Jericho,
> Zacchaeus, an extremely rich and influential tax collector,
> Tried to get a look at Jesus, but he couldn't

See over the crowds on the road side.
Zacchaeus ran ahead and climbed up into a sycamore tree;
    When Jesus passed that way, He looked at him and said,
    "Zachaeus, come down, I'm going to eat at your home."
Zacchaeus hurriedly came down and prepared a banquet for Jesus,
    But the crowd disapproved because Zachaeus was a
    Backslidden Jewish tax collector.
Zacchaeus told Jesus, "I will give half my wealth
    To the poor, and those I've cheated; I will restore
    Four times what I took from them."
Jesus said, "Today salvation has come to this house
    Because he is a son of Abraham.
"The Son of Man has come to seek and save
    Those who are lost, such as Zacchaeus."

Some thought the Kingdom would come immediately,
    So Jesus told a parable to correct that wrong impression.
"A noble man was called to a distant place,
    To be crowned king of that province.
"Before he left, he called his ten workers and gave them
    Each $2,000 to invest while he was gone.
"But some of the workers rebelled and sent the nobleman
    Word that he was no longer their lord and king.
"When the nobleman returned, he called the workers
    To whom he had given money to find out their profit.
"The first man reported his $2,000 had made a profit
    Of $20,000, ten times the original amount.
"'Wonderful,' responded the nobleman, 'you have been faithful;
    You will be ruler of 10 cities.'
"The second worker reported he had turned his $2,000
    Into $10,000, five times the original amount;
    The nobleman made him ruler of five cities.
"The third man had only the original $2,000, so he explained,
    'Because you are an exacting man, reaping

Where you don't sow, I was afraid.
I hid it safely in linen cloth.'
"The nobleman called him a 'wicked worker,' saying,
'You are condemned by your own words.
"'You knew I reaped where I didn't sow, therefore,
Why didn't you deposit my money in a bank,
So I could have drawn interest from it?'"
"The nobleman said to those standing near, 'Take the $2,000
From him and give it to the man with $20,000';
They answered the nobleman, 'He already has $20,000.'"
Jesus answered, "Those who do more with more, will get even more,
And those who do little with little, it shall be taken from him."

Lord, make me faithful with what I have
Use me even in a greater way in the future.

The Anointing at Bethany

Matthew 26:6-13; Mark 14:3-9; John 12:1-9

Lord, I worship Jesus for His death for my sins,
Just as Mary worshiped Him at the feast at Bethany.

Six days before the Passover meal, Jesus attended a banquet
At the home of Martha in Bethany;
Lazarus her brother sat with Jesus at the head of the table.
Mary poured a jar of costly spikard perfume
Over the feet of Jesus and wiped them with her hair;
The house filled with the beautiful smell.
Judas Iscariot complained that the perfume could be sold
And the fortune given to care for the poor.
Not that he cared for the poor, but he was a thief
Who was in charge of the money given to Jesus.
Jesus answered, "Let her alone, she is preparing me

For burial. You can help the poor later,
But you won't have Me very long."
When the crowds heard that Jesus had come to Jerusalem,
They came eagerly to see Him and Lazarus;
The one who Jesus raised from the dead.
Then the religious leaders decided to kill Lazarus also,
Because many believed on Jesus because of Lazarus.

Lord, because I believe Jesus is the Son of God
I give to Him the perfume of my worship.

Part Three

JESUS—THE REDEEMER

Chapter 14

JESUS IN JERUSALEM

The Story of the Triumphant Entry into Jerusalem

In the days leading to the feast of Passover, the word on the streets was that the chief priest planned to arrest Jesus if He dared to show Himself in Jerusalem. Because of this, many said, "Jesus will not come to Jerusalem. It is too dangerous for Him here." Others argued that if Jesus were truly the Messiah, He had nothing to fear.

The Pharisees and priests fully expected the Nazarene to come, and were prepared to seize Him before He could enter the temple. "If anyone knows where He is staying," the priests told their spies, "report it immediately so that we might arrest Him."

Early Sunday morning, the day after the Sabbath, many of His followers went ahead of Jesus into Jerusalem to spread news of His coming. Thousands gathered at the city gate to see if the one they called Messiah would indeed come to the city.

Jesus and the Twelve departed Bethany. As they came near to a village, Jesus instructed Peter and John, saying, "Go to the village ahead of you. Just as you enter, you will find a donkey with a colt which no one has ever ridden. Untie it and bring it here."

Jesus said to them, "If anyone asks you, 'Why are you taking this animal?' tell him, 'The Lord has need of the donkey and will send it back.'"

As Peter and John entered the village, they spotted a young donkey. Without hesitation, they began to lead it away. The owner of the donkey ran after them, shouting, "Where are you going with my colt?"

Peter said, "The Lord has need of the donkey and will send it back shortly."

Leading the donkey to Jesus, Peter and John removed their tunics to drape them over the animal for Jesus to ride upon. Jesus sat upon the colt. Resuming their ascent of Olivet, the apostles broke into a psalm of praise. "Open to me the gates of righteousness. I will go through them and praise the Lord," they sang.

The apostles marched victoriously, moved by the excitement of the crowd. When the procession swept over the ridge, the city of Jerusalem loomed before them.

Thousands of people had lined the road leading into Jerusalem to greet Jesus. Many had spread their cloaks on the road, while others cut palm branches for the festive occasion.

The crowds ahead of Him picked up the refrain of those who followed, shouting, "Hosanna to the Son of David! Blessed is He who comes in the name of the Lord!"

The apostles were caught up in the excitement and did not notice that Jesus was untouched by the enthusiasm. A single tear fell down His face as He stared at the city that had rejected Him. Jesus said quietly, "O Jerusalem, if you only knew…. The day will come when your enemies will trample down your walls, because you did not recognize the time of God's coming to you."

There was no chance the religious leaders could arrest Jesus when He was surrounded by so many supporters. Still, one of them forced his way into the road to confront Jesus. With agitation in his voice, he said, "Teacher, rebuke Your disciples! They are out of control!"

Jesus now turned from His disciples and smiled broadly. He looked down on the Pharisee and said, laughing, "If they were to keep quiet, the stones would cry out in their place."

Jesus rode the donkey through the gate and into the narrow streets of the city. There He dismounted and looked about Him as the people cheered ever louder. Within days, these who worshiped Him would turn fickle and shout for His death. But today their voices would not be silenced.

The Triumphant Entry

Matthew 21:4-9; Mark 11:7-10; Luke 19:35-38; John 12:12-19

Lord, I gladly receive the presence of Jesus into my life
Just as the crowds received Jesus on Palm Sunday.

The next day—Sunday—news that Jesus was coming to Jerusalem
   Swept through the crowds of Passover pilgrims.
As Jesus came to Bethpage, He sent two disciples
   Into the village, telling them they would find
   A donkey with her young colt tied there.
"If any one asks why you are taking the donkey,
   Tell them the Master needs it to ride into Jerusalem."
This act fulfilled Scripture, "Tell the people of Zion,
   Your king is coming to you, humbly riding on a donkey,
   Even on a young colt."
The disciples did as instructed and found the donkey as Jesus said,
   They put their coats on the donkey and Jesus rode on him,
   On a colt that had never been ridden by anyone.
Great crowds spread their coats on the road,
   Others waved their palm branches as they went to meet Him.
The crowds who marched in front of Jesus shouted,
   "Hosanna to the Son of David,
   Blessing on Him who comes in the Lord's name,
   Hosanna in the highest Heaven."
The religious ruler said to Jesus, "Rebuke Your followers,
   For they are blaspheming God and the Scriptures."

Jesus answered them, "If they stopped praising God,

The rocks would immediately cry out praise to God."

The religious rulers said among themselves,

"The whole world is following Him."

When Jesus entered the city, people everywhere were asking,

"Who is this?"

The multitude answered, "This is Jesus, the prophet from Nazareth."

Cursing the Barren Fig Tree and Cleansing the Temple

Matthew 21:12-19; Mark 11:12-18; Luke 19:45-48

The following morning, Jesus left Bethany and was hungry,

He saw a fig tree with leaves but

There were no figs for Him to eat.

Jesus said, "You'll never bear fruit again";

The disciples heard and made a mental note of it.

When Jesus got to the temple, He began cleansing it;

He forced the merchants and their customers to leave,

Then He upset the tables of those selling pigeons,

And stopped workers from bringing in their merchandise.

Jesus said, "Do not the Scriptures teach, 'My house

Shall be called a house of prayer for all people,

But it's become a den of thieves?'"

The religious leaders heard what Jesus said

But they were afraid to do anything against Jesus,

Because the people were listening intently to Him.

Lord I love You for the truth You teach me

Even when the world hates You and Your truth.

The Greeks Want To See Jesus

John 12:20-50

There were some Greeks worshiping in the temple;
       They approached Philip asking, "We would like
       To see Jesus," Philip told Andrew and they told Jesus.
Jesus didn't answer directly but said,
       "The hour has come
       For the Son of Man to return to Heaven and be glorified.
"A grain of wheat must die when it falls to the ground,
       Otherwise it will remain only one grain of wheat.
"But if it dies, it yields a rich harvest of food,
       Those who love their life will lose it
       And those who don't live for this life
       Will exchange it for eternal life.
"If anyone wants to be My disciples, including the Greeks,
       They must follow Me, then they will be where I am
       And the Father will honor them when they follow Me.
"Now my soul is greatly troubled. Shall I ask
       My Father to deliver Me from the house of suffering?
"No! That is the purpose why I came to earth;
       Father, glorify Your name through My coming death."
Then they heard a voice from Heaven, "I have glorified it, and
       I will glorify it again."
Some who heard it thought it was thunder,
       Others thought it was an angel speaking.
Jesus answered, "This sound was for your sake, not Mine,
       The time for judgment of sin has come,
       Satan—the prince of the world—will be cast out.
"When I am lifted up—on the Cross—I will draw all to Me";
       Jesus said this to predict the way He would die.
The crowd was astonished answering, "We thought
       The Scriptures taught Messiah would live forever.

"Why are You saying the Son of Man must be lifted up in death?
  Are You talking about the Messiah?"
Jesus said, "My light will illuminate you only a short time,
  Learn from the light while you can
  Or else darkness will fall and you'll be lost in it.
"While you have the light, believe the light.
  And you'll become children of the light";
  Then Jesus left and they couldn't find Him.

Despite all the miracles Jesus did, most of the people
  Did not believe Jesus was the predicted Messiah.
This fulfilled the prediction of Isaiah who said,
  "Lord they don't believe, they don't accept Your miracles."
Indeed, they couldn't believe, as Isaiah said in another place,
  "God has blinded their eyes and hardened their hearts,
  Lest they should see with their eyes and understand with their
  Hearts, and turn to God and He saves them."

Nevertheless, many leading citizens believed on Jesus,
  But they didn't confess Him openly for fear of social pressure.
They were afraid of being excommunicated from the temple
  For they desired acceptance by people, more than from God.

Jesus proclaimed loudly in the temple, "Those believing in Me,
  Also believe in the Father who sent Me.
"And those who understand what I am saying,
  Also understand what the Father wants them to know.
"I have come as a light to all people,
  And those who believe in Me will not live in darkness.
"If anyone hears and understands My teachings, but rejects them,
  I will not judge them for I come to save all people.
"But those who do not accept my teachings and reject Me,
  Will be judged in the last day by what I've said;
  The Father will judge him.
"Because the Father who sent Me told Me what to say

And His words give life eternal.
"Therefore everything I am saying to you
Comes from the Father in Heaven."

Lord, I believe in You and will obey Your words,
For I know they give me eternal life.

The Withered Fig Tree

Matthew 21:19-22; Mark 11:19-25; Luke 21:37,38

During the Passover week Jesus stayed in Bethany;
On Tuesday morning Jesus and the disciples saw that the fig tree
He had cursed the previous day was dead and withered.
Peter was amazed that the tree had withered to its roots;
Jesus answered, "Let God's faith control you.
"Verily, if you will say to a mountain,
'Be removed and thrown in the sea' and you don't doubt,
But believe that you will receive what you ask,
You shall have it."
Jesus then explained, "You shall have all things for which you ask
If you believe before you receive them."

Jesus then instructed, "When you begin to pray,
You must forgive those you have an issue with,
So that you Father may forgive your sin,
Then you have a basis for getting an answer to prayer."

Lord, I forgive those who sin against me and I want You
To forgive me for my wrong feelings against any.
Forgive me of all my sins so You can
Answer my prayers.

A Day of Controversy in the Temple

Matthew 21:23–22:14; Mark 11:27–12:12; Luke 20:1-19

As Jesus entered the temple, the chief priest and scribe
　　Asked Him, "By what authority are you doing these things?"
Jesus responded, "I will ask you one question, and what you say
　　Will answer your question to Me.
"Did John the Baptist get his authority from Heaven or men?"
　　They realized that if they said, "From God"
　　Jesus would ask why they didn't receive Him.
They also realized that if they said "From men,"
　　They would upset the multitude
　　For they believed John the Baptist was from God.
So the religious leaders answered Jesus, "We don't know";
　　Then Jesus said, "Neither will I answer you
　　Where I get My authority."

Jesus told a parable of a Father who had two sons,
　　He said to the first, "Son, go work today in the vineyard,
　　The son said, "I will not go," but later repented and went.
The father said the same thing to the second son,
　　He answered, "I will go," but he didn't do it, and
Then Jesus asked, "Which son did the Father's will?"
　　The leaders answered, "The first." Jesus answered,
　　"Sinners and rebels who repent will go into the Kingdom
　　Before you because they do the will of the Father.
"John the Baptist preached the way of righteousness,
　　But you did not believe him, so you rebelled against the Father,
　　Yet sinners responded to his message and entered the Kingdom."

Then Jesus told them another parable of a landowner
　　Who planted a vineyard, planted a hedge to protect it,
　　Built a tower and winepress, then rented it out
　　To renters and moved away.

When the harvest of grapes came, the landowner sent for the rent
 That would come from the harvest.
The renters beat the first to collect the rent,
 Stoned another, and killed the next one;
 When the landowner sent more to collect, they did the same
Then the landowner said, "The renters will reverence my son,"
 But the renters conspired, "The son will get
 The vineyard as an inheritance. Let's kill him
 So we will get the vineyard." And they did it.
When the owner heard what the renters did, he
 Destroyed the miserable renters
 Then he rented out the vineyard to other renters.
This is a picture of the Father giving the Promised Land
 To the Jews, but they rejected the prophets
 So the Jews were punished by God.
The Father then turned His attention to different people,
 The Gospel was presented to the Gentiles.
Jesus said, "The stone which the builders rejected
 Became the most useful and prominent stone of all;
 Then you'll marvel at what God does."

Jesus told yet another parable that the kingdom of God
 Was likened to a king planning a marriage feast for his son;
 He sent messengers to call those who were invited,
 But they wouldn't come.
Again, the king sent messengers telling them the best beef
 Is being cooked, and everything is on the table
 But they made light of the king's invitation.
One guest went to his farm, another opened his store for business,
 The other guest beat the king's messengers, killing some.
The king was angry and sent his army to kill the murderers
 And destroy their cities.
The king told his messengers, "The marriage feast is ready
 And those I invited were not worthy to attend.

"Go to the country roads, and invite everyone that you see
        To come to the marriage feast for my son."
The servants did as the king commanded and invited
        Both the good and the bad and the wedding was filled.
But when the king entered the banquet hall,
        He saw a man without wedding garments.
The king said, "Why aren't you wearing wedding clothes?"
        The man couldn't answer the king.
The king told his servants to bind the man and
        Cast him into outer darkness where
        There is weeping, wailing, and gnashing of teeth.
This means the Jews who were originally God's people,
        Like the invited guests, refused God's invitation
        So He aggressively punished them.
Those who came from the country roads are the Gentiles
        Who responded to God's grace.
The man without wedding garments represents those
        Who know about God's offer, but haven't received Christ,
        So they are not dressed in the garments of righteousness.

Lord, I believe You and have been justified by faith;
        I look forward to the marriage supper of the Lamb.

The Pharisees' and Herodians' Question

Matthew 22:15-22; Mark 12:13-17; Luke 20:20-26

Still in the temple, some Pharisees and Herodians tried to
        Trip up Jesus with the issue of bringing Roman coins
        Into the temple with an image of Caesar.
Since Caesar considered himself God, this broke the
        Law about possessing images of a god.
They said, "Master, we know You stand for the truth,
        And you teach the truth, no matter who is listening to You,

Should we pay taxes to Caesar?"
    If Jesus said "no," they'd accuse Him of insurrection.
Jesus knew their evil plan, so He said, "Show me a coin";
    They had broken the law by having a coin in the temple.
Jesus said, "Hypocrites, whose image is on this coin?"
    They answered, "Caesar's."
Jesus answered them, "Give to Caesar the things that are Caesar's,
    And give to God the things that are God's";
    They marveled at Jesus' wisdom, and left Him alone.

The Sadducees' Question

Matthew 22:23-33; Mark 12:18-27; Luke 20:27-40

The Sadducees, who deny the resurrection, came to Jesus
    With a question about the resurrection.
"Master, a man married a woman and they had no children,
    If he dies and his brother marries her,
    So that the legal line continues...
"Then the same thing happens seven more times, so that
    She has had seven husbands...in the resurrection,
    Whose wife of the seven shall she be?"
Jesus answered, "You are basically wrong in your understanding
    Of the Scriptures and the power of God.
"In the resurrection, people are not married nor do they get married;
    And they won't die again, but they are like angels
    They possess eternal life.
"When Moses met God at the burning bush, God said
    'I am the God of Abraham, Isaac, and Jacob.'
"If there were no resurrection, God would have said,
    I was their God. But because they had a future hope,
    Even though dead, God was their God at that time."

Some other religious leaders told Jesus He gave

A good answer to the Sadducees.

Lord, I believe in the resurrection and I know I

Will be raised because I now live in Jesus Christ.

A Legal Question

Matthew 22:34-40; Mark 12:28-34

A lawyer next tried to trip up Jesus, asking, "Master

What is the greatest law in the commandments?"

Jesus answered, "You shall love the Lord your God,

With all your heart, with all your soul,

With all your mind, and with all your strength.

"The second which is like unto it, 'You shall love

Your neighbor as yourself.'"

The lawyer replied, "Master, You spoke correctly,

There is only one God, and none other than He;

And that we should love Him with all our hearts,

With all our understanding, with all our strength."

"And to love our neighbors as ourselves. All this is greater

Than offering burnt offerings and sacrifices."

Jesus noticed he answered sincerely and said,

"You are not far from the kingdom of God."

As a result, no other religious leaders questioned Jesus

Because they were afraid of being embarrassed by Him.

Lord, I trust every answer You have to all my questions.

Now Jesus Asks a Question

Matthew 22:41-46; Mark 12:35-37; Luke 20:41-44

Since the religious leaders had no more questions,
>Jesus then asked them, "You scribes say that
>Messiah—Christ—is the son of David.
"Yet David himself said, 'The Lord said to my Lord,
>Sit on my right hand till I make
>Your enemies a foot stool for Your feet.'
"Since David called Messiah his Lord
>How can Messiah be His son?"
No one was able to answer Jesus and
>No one wanted to debate Him.

Jesus Denounces Scribes and Pharisees

Matthew 23:1-39; Mark 12:38-40; Luke 20:45-47

After a while, Jesus went into the courtyard
>Of the temple to teach the multitudes,
"Beware of the scribes, who like to sit in Moses' seat
>They make rules for you to obey, but they themselves
>Do not obey their own rules.
"They put heavy and grievous burdens on your shoulders,
>But they will not bear them, nor
>Will they lift one finger to help you.
"They love to wear long robes to get greetings from everyone,
>They love the best seats at the feast and in the synagogues."

"Woe to you scribes and Pharisees—hypocrites—because
>You shut the door to the kingdom of God
>And you yourselves will not enter,
>Nor will you let anyone else enter.

"Woe to you scribes and Pharisees—hypocrites—because
      You go everywhere to make people your proselyte,
      Yet you make him a two-fold son of hell.
"Because he was originally on his way to hell,
      Now as your proselyte he is doubly directed to hell.
"Woe to you blind guides, you say it is alright
      To swear by the temple, but not by the gold on the temple;
      You're fools, what is greater, the temple or the gold?
"You say it is alright to swear by the altar,
      But it's not right to swear by the gift on the altar;
      You're blind, what is greater the altar or the sacrifice?
"If you swear by the heavens, you also swear by
      The throne of God, and by Him who sits on the throne.
"Woe to you scribes and Pharisees—hypocrites—you are careful to
      Tithe the mint that grows out your back door, but
      You've left undone the weightier things of the law
      Which is judgment, and self-control, and faith.
"It's right to tithe everything God gives to you,
      But it's wrong to ignore those greater things;
      You strain at a gnat and swallow a camel.
"Woe to you scribes and Pharisees—hypocrites—because
      You clean the outside of the cup, but leave the inside filthy.
"Woe to you scribes and Pharisees—hypocrites—because
      You're like a freshly painted grave that looks beautiful,
      But inwardly you're dead, rotting, stinking corpses.
"Outwardly, you appear to people to be righteous,
      But inwardly, you're full of sin and hypocrisy."
"Woe to you scribes and Pharisees—hypocrites—because
      You build monuments at the tombs of the prophets,
      And you make a big spectacle of putting flowers on their graves.
"Yet if you lived in their day, you'd be
      Part of those who killed them.
"You are serpents and children of snakes,

How will you escape the punishment of hell?"
"You are just like those to whom the Father sent prophets
    To preach to them. Yet you would scourge them,
    Persecute them and crucify them.
"And on your hands is the blood of all righteous martyrs,
    From the blood of Abel to the blood of Zechariah
    Who was killed in the temple next to the altar."

"O Jerusalem, Jerusalem who killed the prophets and
    Stoned those who were sent to you from the Father.
"How often would I have gathered you to Me, as a hen gathers her chicks,
    But you would not come to Me.
"You will not see Me or understand what I am doing in the world,
    Till I come again in the name of the Lord."

Then Jesus went to sit by the place where
    Money offerings were made to God.
The rich poured in much money, and the people applauded;
    No one noticed a poor widow giving two small coins.
Jesus said to His disciples, "Verily, this woman
    Has given more than all the others
    Because they gave out of their abundance,
    But she gave all that she had."

Lord, I give You all that I have, not for the applause of people,
    But because You gave all that You had—Your life—for me.

The Mount of Olives Discourse

Matthew 24 and 25; Mark 13:1-37; Luke 21:5-36

Later in the day—Tuesday—Jesus sat
    With His disciples on the Mount of Olives
    To look at the city of Jerusalem and the temple.
Jesus said, "You see the city and temple, verily not one stone

Will be left on another, but shall be thrown down."
His disciples asked Jesus privately, "Tell us when this
 Will happen? And what shall be the sign of Your coming?
 And what shall be the sign of the end of the world?"
Jesus answered, "Don't let anyone lead you astray, because
 Many will come in my name, saying, 'I am the Christ!'
"You will hear of wars and rumors of wars, but don't worry
 Because these things must happen before the end."
"Nation will fight nation, and alliances of nations will fight
 Other alliances; and there will be earthquakes;
 These are the beginning of hard tribulations.
"Your enemy will arrest you, persecute you, and kill you,
 All nations will hate the nation of Israel for my sake.
"Many false prophets will lead astray many, and the influence
 Of sin will influence every area of life
 And love for Me will become cold.
"But those followers of Mine who endure tribulation to the end,
 They shall be finally saved.
"The Gospel of the Kingdom will be preached to the whole world
 Then the end shall come."

"When you see the abomination of desolation—a pig
 Sacrificed on the altar—which was predicted by Daniel,
 Realize this is the beginning of the Great Tribulation.
"Then let my people flee to the mountains for protection,
 Let those on the roof top not go in their house
 To take anything with them.
"Let those working in the field not return home for clothes,
 And those with child will suffer the most;
 And pray your escape is not in winter or on the Sabbath.
"This will be the Great Tribulation which is greater than any
 Since the beginning of the world and greater than any after it.
"Except God shortening these days, no one can live through it,
 And for God's people, those days will be shortened.

"If anyone tells you, 'Here is the Messiah, or there is the Messiah,'
     Don't believe it, because many false Messiahs
     Will come and perform miracles to lead away God's people.
"If anyone tells you Messiah is in the wilderness,
     Don't go out there to check it out. And if they say
     Messiah is in an inner room, don't believe it either.
"Because the coming of the Son of Man will be as spectacular
     As lightening flashing from the East to the West.
"And there'll be so many slain by His coming, that the buzzard
     Will gather to eat their flesh.
"The sun will be darkened and the moon won't shine,
     And stars will fall from the sky, and Heaven itself
     Will be shaken as the Son of Man makes
     His appearance in Heaven.
"Then shall all ethnic tribes mourn when they see Him,
     Coming with great power and glory through the clouds.
"He will send His angels with the sound of a trumpet
     To gather His people from the four corners of the earth."

"Learn from the parable of the fig tree, when new growth
     Appears and the leaves are growing, realize it is summer;
     So when you see these signs happening, Messiah is at the door.
"This generation of Jewish believers will not pass away
     Until all these signs have appeared.
"Heaven and earth shall pass away, but My Word—which I promise—
     shall not pass away, but these things will happen as promised.
"But no one knows the hour when Messiah will come, not
     You, nor anyone else, or even the angels in Heaven, neither
     The Son of Man, but only the Father knows the hour.
"It will be like the days of Noah. He warned everyone that
     Judgment was coming. But no one believed him, they went on
     Eating, getting drunk, getting married until the flood came.
"Two will be working in the field, one will be taken, the other left.

Two women will be grinding meal, one will be taken, the other left;
Watch because you don't know when He will return."

Lord, I expect You to come at any minute.

"If the owner of the house knew when a thief would
    Break into his home, he would have been constantly vigilant.
"Therefore, be ready for in just the hour you think He won't return,
    He will come.
"If the owner made a faithful worker supervisor
    Of all his businesses while he was gone, that worker is blessed
    If the owner returns to find everything in order.
"Verily, the owner would give him a promotion,
    But if the servant is lazy and spends his time eating and drinking
    Because he thinks the owner is tarrying,
"The owner will come back at a time the worker doesn't expect him,
    And will fire the worker and give his job to someone else;
    The worker will suffer with those who weep and gnash
    Their Teeth."

Jesus spoke a parable that the coming of the Kingdom is likened to
    "Ten bridesmaids with ten lamps
    Who were waiting for the coming of the bridegroom.
"Five foolish bridesmaids didn't take oil with them
    But five wise bridesmaids took oil in addition to their lamps.
"The bridegroom was late and all the bridesmaids slept;
    At midnight there was a shout, 'He's coming!
    Let all the bridesmaids come meet him.'
"When the ten lit their lamps, the five foolish asked the wise,
    'Give us some oil because our lamps are going out.'
"But the wise answered, 'If we give you some of ours,
    We won't have enough to light the bridegroom's way';
    They told the foolish virgins to go buy some for themselves.
"The five wise virgins went into the feast, with
    The bridegroom and the door was shut.

"Afterward the five foolish virgins came asking, 'Open the door,'
  But the bridegroom answered, "I don't know you.""

Lord, I will watch constantly for Your return, because
  I don't know the day or hour that You're coming.

Jesus spoke another parable about His returning, saying,
  "A businessman planned to take a long trip,
  And delegated to various workers, different jobs in the company.
"He gave one worker $500,000, another $200,000
  And the third $100,000; each according to his ability
  To manage money.
"The one with $500,000 invested wisely and doubled his money;
  The one with $200,000 also invested prudently and doubled his money.
"The worker with $100,000 hid his money carefully so it wouldn't be lost;
  After a long time, the boss returned and
  Asked his workers to report what they had done.
"The one who had $500,000 brought in another $500,000,
  The boss said, 'You've done well because you were faithful,
  I'm going to promote you to a larger responsibility.'"

Lord, like this worker I want Your approval.

"The one with $200,000 gave the owner an additional $200,000;
  The boss also said congratulations and promoted the second Worker.
"The worker with $100,000 said, 'I know you are a hard man,
  Reaping where you don't sow, and I was afraid
  So I safely hid your money, and here it is!'
"The owner said, 'You're a lazy worker. You know I expected
  Profit from my investment. You should have put it
  In a bank where it would earn interest.'
"The owner took away the $100,000 and gave it to the
  Worker that now had a million dollars."
Jesus said, "If you have gathered much for the Kingdom
  You'll be given more. If you've done little

For the Kingdom, it'll be taken from you.
"The owner said, 'Cast the unprofitable servant into outer darkness,
    Where there is weeping and gnashing of teeth.'"

Jesus explained, "When you see the Son of Man come
    In His glory, you'll see before Him all the
    Nations of the earth.
"The Son of Man will sit on His throne to divide them
    As a shepherd divides his flock;
    Sheep will be separated to His right hand, and goats to the left.
"Then the king will say to those on the right, 'Come in
    Because you are blessed, inherit the Kingdom prepared for you.'"
Then Jesus will say to them, "You are blessed because I was
    Hungry and you fed Me. I was thirsty and you gave Me drink,
    I was naked and you took Me in. I was in prison
    And you came and visited Me.
"Those on the right said, 'When did we see You hungry,
    Or thirsty, or naked, or in prison?'
"The king shall answer, 'Inasmuch as you did it
    To my brethren and the poor, you did it to Me.'
"Then the king will say to those on the left, 'Depart
    From Me into eternal fire prepared for the devil and his demons.'"

Lord, give me a compassion for needy brethren and the poor,
    May I do good works in service to You.

Events on Wednesday

Matthew 26:1-16; Mark 14:1-11; Luke 22:1-6

On Wednesday Jesus said to His disciples,
    "In two days the Son of Man will be delivered up to be crucified."

The religious leaders with Caiaphas the High Priest came together
    To discuss how to arrest Jesus and kill Him.

But they decided not to do it during Passover,
      Lest there be an uprising among the people.

That night Jesus attended a feast in Bethany in the home
      Of Simon the leper.
A woman poured a pound of alabaster from a jar
      On Jesus' head. The oil was very costly.
Some in the crowd were indignant, thinking the ointment
      Was wasted. They wanted to sell it and give
      The money to the poor.
Jesus understood what they were saying, so He answered,
      "Why are you criticizing the woman? She has done
      A good work on Me.
"You always will have the poor, and you can do for them
      What you want to do. But you won't always have Me;
      She has anointed My body for its burial.
"Wherever the Gospel is preached in the world,
      She will be remembered for her act of worship."

One of the Twelve—Judas Iscariot—went to the chief priest
      And asked, "What will you give me if I deliver Jesus to you?"
      The religious rulers gave him 30 pieces of silver,
      So Judas looked for an opportunity to deliver Jesus to them.

Events on Thursday

Matthew 26:17-19; Mark 14:12-16; Luke 22:7-13

On Thursday, the day when the Passover lamb was killed,
      The disciples asked Jesus, "Where do You want to celebrate Passover?"
      Jesus told Peter and John to go in the city and find a man
      With a pitcher on his head. "Follow him to a house,
      And ask the owner for a room where I can celebrate Passover.
"He will show you a larger upper room, get it ready

For Me to celebrate the Passover."
And they went and found the man just as Jesus said,
And they prepared it for the Passover meal.

The Last Supper

Matthew 26:20-30; Mark 14:17-26; Luke 22:14-30; John 13:1-29

And when evening was come, Jesus sat with His disciples and said
"I have a great desire to eat this meal with you before I suffer.
I will not eat with you again until we eat in the kingdom of God."

The disciples began arguing who was the greatest. Jesus said,
"The Gentiles have kings who exercise authority over them
But you should not be like them.
"He that is greatest, let him be the servant of the least;
Who is greater, those who sit to eat, or those who serve?
I am among you as One who serves.
"But you are those who have been with me since my temptation,
I will give you part of the Kingdom My Father gives me.
"You will sit to eat and drink at my table in the Kingdom,
And sit on twelve thrones ruling the twelve tribes of Israel."

Jesus knew that His time had come to leave the world
Because Judas Iscariot had already betrayed Him
And having loved His own, He loved them to the end.
Knowing that the Father had put all things into His hand
That He had come from the Father and would return to Him,
He arose from the table, laid aside His tunic, and
Wrapped a towel around Himself as a servant.
He poured water into the basin, began washing the disciples' feet
And wiping them dry with the towel.

When Jesus came to Peter, the fisherman asked, "Will You
  Wash my feet?" Jesus answered, "You don't
  Understand now, but you'll understand in the future.
"If I don't wash you,
  You'll have no part with Me."
But Peter answered the Lord, "If that's the case, then
  Not only my feet, but my hands and head."
Jesus answered, "He that is bathed all over,
  Need only to have his feet washed;
  Now you are clean, but not all of you."
For Jesus knew who would betray him, therefore He said,
  "You are not all clean."

When Jesus finished washing their feet, He put His tunic back on
  And sat down with them and said, "Do you know
  What I have done for you?
"You call Me Master and Lord, and so I am. If I then
  Your Lord and Master have washed your feet,
  Then you ought to be willing to wash one another's feet.
"I have given you the example to do to others
  What I have done for you."

"Verily, verily I say to you, a servant is not greater than his master,
  Neither is the one sent greater than the one who sent him;
  If you know these things, happy are you if you do them.
"I have chosen all of you, but not all are of Me,
  That the Scriptures may be fulfilled, 'He that eats
  With Me, lifts up his heel against Me.'
"I'm telling you before it happens, so when it comes to pass,
  You will know I am your Messiah."

Jesus was obviously troubled, then he said, "Verily, verily
  I say to you, one of you will betray me."
The disciples looked at one another, not completely
  Understanding what Jesus meant. Then each one

Said, "Lord, is it I?"
Jesus answered, "He that dips his hand in the same dish
    That I dip, he is the one who will betray me;
    It is good if that man were never born."
John was reclining on Jesus' shoulder. Peter beckoned
    For John to find out who Jesus meant.
Jesus answered, "When I dip the bread into the lamb stew,
    The one to whom I give it is the one."
Then Jesus dipped the bread into the stew and gave it to Judas,
    But the disciples didn't understand
    Because Judas was the honored guest,
    And it was the custom to give it to that person first.
After Judas received the bread, satan entered in him;
    Jesus said to him, "Do quickly what you are going to do."
None of the disciples understood what happened because they
    Thought Jesus said, "Buy what is needed
    For the Passover feast."
When Judas received the bread, he went out into the darkness;
    The night was truly black.

Lord, may I never betray You with any deeds,
    Thought or attitudes.

Jesus and Peter

Matthew 26:31-35; Mark 14:27-31; Luke 22:31-38; John 13:30-38

When Judas left, Jesus was relieved saying, "Now is
    The Son of Man glorified and God is glorified.
"Children, I am going to be with you only a short time;
    You'll look for Me and can't find Me because where I'm going
    You cannot follow Me now."
"So, I'm giving you a new commandment that you

254

Love one another as I have loved you."
Peter asked, "Where are you going?" The Lord answered, "You cannot
    Now go where I am going,
    But later you can follow Me."
Peter answered, "Why can I not follow You?
    I will lay down my life for Your sake."
Jesus replied, "You only think you'll die for Me. Verily, verily,
    I say to you, you will deny Me three times
    Before the rooster crows."

Institution of the Lord's Table

Matthew 26:26-29; Mark 14:22-25; Luke 22:12-20; 1 Corinthians 11:23-26

As they were eating, Jesus took bread, blessed it and said,
    "This is my body which is broken for you,
    Eat this in remembrance of Me."
And Jesus took the cup and gave thanks and said,
    "This cup symbolizes the new agreement by God
    To forgive your sins by My blood.
"For as often as you eat this bread and drink this
    Cup, you are demonstrating your salvation
    And you should do it till I come again."

The Upper Room Discourse

John 14:1-31

Jesus told the eleven, "Do not let your heart be troubled,
    Hold on to your faith in God and your faith in Me.
"There are many rooms in my Father's house,
    If it were not true, I would have told you.

"I am going to prepare a place there for you,
    And when I get it ready, I will come back for you,
    Then I'll take you to be with Me.
"You know the way to the place I am going,
    But Thomas responded, "No! We don't know where
    You are going, nor do we know how to get there."
Jesus said, "I am the way to Heaven, also the
    Truth and eternal life. You must come through
    Me to go to the Father.
"Since you know Me, you should also know the Father,
    And from now on you'll know the Father."
Philip disagreed, "We don't know what the Father looks like,
    Show us the Father so we can believe."
Jesus answered, "I have been with you all this time,
    And you don't know Me;
    He who has seen Me has seen the Father.
"What I say are not My words, but
    They are from the Father who lives in Me;
    The Father also does the miracles that I do.
"Believe that I am in the Father, and He is in Me,
    Or else, believe it because you have seen My miracles.
"Verily, verily, I say to you, he that believeth in Me shall do
    The works that I do, and even greater ones,
    Because I am going to the Father.
"Whatever you pray in My name, I'll do it
    So that the Father will be glorified in Me;
    If you pray for anything in My name, I'll do it."

Lord, give me faith to pray for greater miracles
    Than I'll ever expect and I'll give You the glory.

Jesus told them, "If you love Me, obey the commandments,
    And I will ask the Father to send you
    Another person in My place. He will live in you forever.

"This other person is the Holy Spirit, the third person of the Trinity,
  The unsaved cannot receive Him, because they
  Do not believe in Him or know anything about Him.
"But you will know the Holy Spirit because you believe in Me;
  He has been with you, and shall be in you.
"I will not leave you alone in the world, I will come to you;
  Shortly I will leave you because I'm leaving the world
But you will have Me when I'm gone;
  Because I live, you shall live also.
"At that time you'll know I'm with the Father in Heaven,
  But I'll be in you and you'll be in Me."

"Those who have and keep my commandments are the ones loving Me,
  And those who love Me will be loved by the Father
  And I will love them and I'll show Myself to them."

Lord, I love You will all my heart, take away all blindness
Help me to see You completely and obey You.

Judas—not Iscariot—but another disciple with that name
  Asked, "How can You show Yourself to us
  And not to the world?"
Jesus answered, "Those who love me will obey My commandments,
  And my Father will love them, and
  We will come to live in them.
"Those who don't obey My commandments don't love Me.
  It's not just my Word they reject; it's the Father's Word.
"I am explaining these things to you while I'm with you,
  But the Holy Spirit, whom the Father will send in My place,
  He'll explain all spiritual things to you,
  And will remind you of the things I said to you.
"I am leaving My peace with you, not as the world gives,
  So don't be afraid of anything."

"Previously, I told you I am going away but I'm coming back.
　　　Because you love Me, rejoice that I'm going to the Father;
　　　I tell you this before it happens,
　　　So you'll believe in Me when it happens.
"I will not be able to talk with you much more,
　　　The evil prince of this world is coming to try Me
　　　But don't worry, he has no authority over Me.
"I am going to do the thing the Father wants me to do,
　　　That will show my love to Him.
"Now, let's leave this upper room."

Lord, I need the Holy Spirit to make me spiritual and I need Him to
　　　Make me holy.

On the Street

John 15 and 16

Jesus said, "I am the true vine, my Father is the gardener,
　　　He cuts away any branches not growing fruit
　　　And prunes back every branch that has fruit."
Lord, I am a healthy plant by Your words;
　　　I will settle down in Christ as He abides in me.
Just as the branch can't bear fruit except it's attached
　　　To the vine, so I can't produce anything
　　　Unless I'm attached to Christ.
Jesus, you are the vine, I am a branch;
　　　As long as I remain attached to You, and You abide in me,
　　　I will bear plenty of fruit.
Anyone who will not remain attached to Jesus,
　　　Will be collected like dead branches
　　　And thrown into the fire to be burned.
Jesus, when I remain settled in You, and Your words

Remain in me, I can ask what I want
And You'll give it to me.

Father, I want to glorify You by bearing much fruit,
Then everyone will know I'm Your disciple.

As the Father has loved Jesus, so He loves me,
So I'll settle down to rest in His love to me.
I will obey the commandments of Jesus to remain in His love
Just as Jesus kept the Father's love to remain in His love.
Jesus, you told me this so Your joy would rest in me
And my joy would then be perfect.
Jesus, you've commanded me to love one another
Just as You've loved us.
I can't have greater love for others than
To lay down my life for them.
I am a friend of Jesus when I obey His commands;
He no longer calls me His servant
Because a servant doesn't know what his master does.
But I am Jesus' friend because I know what He's doing,
He's doing what the Father told Him to do.
I did not choose Jesus, but He chose me
And commissioned me to go bear fruit.
Now whatever I ask You—Father—in Jesus' name,
You gladly give to me.

Lord Jesus, again You command me to love one another,
Because the world will hate me,
But it hated You long before it hated me.
I do not belong to this world and have separated from it,
Therefore, the world hates me.
I remember what You said, "A servant is not greater
Than his master, since they persecute Jesus,
The world will persecute Me."
They will hate me and persecute me because I'm Jesus' disciple

Because they do not know the Father who sent Jesus.
If Jesus hadn't given the truth, the world wouldn't experience
    The guilt of their sin, but now they have no excuse.
If Jesus hadn't done miracles among them, they
    Would have been blinded in their sins. Now they see
And hate both Jesus and the Father. As written
    In Scriptures, "They hated Jesus without a cause."

Lord, when the Holy Spirit comes—the Spirit of truth—who
    Comes from the Father, He will speak plainly
    To their hearts about Jesus Christ.
Then I can also speak plainly about Jesus for He will
    Speak through me and remove their blindness.
Jesus told us about coming persecution so our faith
    Wouldn't be shaken. They will excommunicate me
    From their assemblies.
There is coming a time when they will kill people like me,
    Thinking they have served God. They'll do this
    Because they don't have true knowledge of Jesus or the Father.
Jesus did not originally tell His disciples about persecution
    Because He was walking among them.
But now that He is going away, they needed to be
    Reinforced, so they wouldn't be shaken when it happened.
Yet, none of His disciples asked, "Where are you going?"
    Because they were distressed that He was leaving.
But it was a good thing for Jesus to go away, because
    If He hadn't left, the Holy Spirit would not have come.
But because Jesus left, He sent the Holy Spirit
    To convict the world of sin, righteousness, and judgment.
He will convict—cause people to see—their sin
    Because they do not believe in Jesus.
He will convict—cause people to see—their lack of righteousness,
    Which will keep them out of Heaven.
He will convict—cause people to see—coming judgment

Because Jesus suffered for them on the Cross.
Then Jesus told what the Holy Spirit will do for believers;
    When He comes—The Spirit of truth—He will reveal
    To us everything that is truth. Then He'll
    Guide us to understand truth.
The Holy Spirit will not be concerned with His own agenda,
    But He will bring glory to Jesus Christ,
    And He will reveal to us things to come.
All the Father's glory also belongs to Jesus,
    This is the glory the Holy Spirit will reveal.

In a little while Jesus will leave His disciples and they will
    See Him no longer in the flesh. But a short time
    Later they will see Him.
The disciples did not understand what Jesus meant
    About leaving them and then coming back to them.
Jesus knew they wanted to question Him, so He said
    Plainly, "In a short time you'll no longer see Me;
    Then a short time later, you'll see Me."
Then Jesus explained, "You will weep when I'm gone,
    But the world will rejoice. But your weeping
    Will be turned to rejoicing.
"It'll be like a woman suffering in childbirth so that
    When the child is born, she forgets about her suffering."
Jesus explained they would be sad, but when they see
    Him again, they would be full of joy,
    A joy that no one could take from them.
When that day comes, they won't have any questions
    They can go directly to the Father with their questions.
Jesus then promised, whatever We ask in His name,
    The Father will give it to us.
Up until then the disciples hadn't prayed in Jesus' name,
    Now we can ask in Jesus' name and we receive
    So that our joy will overflow.

Up until that time Jesus used metaphors and parables
      But the time is coming when He'll speak plainly.
When that day comes—and now is—we can ask the Father
      In Jesus' name, and Jesus will pray to the Father for us.
The Father loves us because we have loved Jesus and
      We know that Jesus came to the world from the Father.
The disciples said, "Now we believe You came from the Father,
      You are not using metaphors. Now we understand."
Jesus said, "You only think you understand. The time is
      Coming when you will be scattered to your homes,
      Leaving Me alone."
Jesus said, "I have told you this so you will have peace;
      In the world you will have trials, but have faith
      I have conquered the world."

Chapter 15

THE PRAYERS OF JESUS

A Prayer to be Glorified

John 17:1-26

After Jesus left the Upper Room, tradition says
    He slipped in the Holy of Holies to pray;
    Since Jesus was God, He would know how to get there.
Jesus lifted His eyes to Heaven and prayed, "Father,
    My hour is come. Glorify Thy Son so I can glorify You.
"That those you have given Me should have eternal life;
    Eternal life is You, the only true God,
    And in Jesus Christ, the One You sent to earth."
Jesus said, "I have glorified You on earth
    And accomplished the work You sent Me to do.
"Now Father, glorify Me with the glory I had in Heaven
    Which I had with You before the world was created."

Lord Jesus, I hear Your passion for Your glory to return.
    Now that You're in Heaven,
    I glorify You for all You are and all You've done.

A Prayer to Keep the Disciples Safe

"I have given Your name to the men You gave me;
    They were Your men and You gave them to Me,
    They have faithfully kept Your Word.

"They know the things You told Me to do
      Because I told them what You said to Me.
"They have received Your Word and they believe it
      And they believe I came from Heaven to do Your will.
"I pray for these disciples, I do not pray for the world;
      I pray for those You have given Me.
"All things that are mine are Yours,
      And I am glorified in these disciples.
"I am no longer in the world, but they are in the world,
      So I pray for them.
"I pray—Holy Father—that You would keep them safe,
      That they may be one, as We are One.
"While I was with them, I kept them—guarded them,
      And not one of them is missing, except the son of perdition who
      Fulfilled Scripture by betraying Me.
"Now I come to You, Father, that they may have joy;
      I have given them Your Word, and the world hates them
      Because they reject the world, even as I am not of the world.
"I am not praying for You to take them out of the world,
      But that You would keep them from the evil one.
"Make them holy by Your Word, Your word is truth;
      I am sending them into the world,
      Even as I was sent into the world.
"I set Myself apart from Heaven for them,
      Now may they be set apart to reach others.
"I am not praying for these disciples only,
      I am praying for those who will believe because of their word."

A Prayer To Be One

Jesus prayed that all believers may be one
      As He and the Father are One;
      "I am in them, as You in Me."

"So that the world may realize You sent Me,
    And You love Me and You love them,
"Father, I want them to be with Me in Heaven,
    That they may see My glory
    That I've had before the foundations of the earth.
"O Father, the world does not know You,
    But I have known You and made You known to these disciples
"That the love You have for Me may be in them,
    And I in them, and they in Me."

Lord, I want to be one with You, You in me and I in You.
    May the world see my love and
    May the world become believers in You.

Jesus' Prayer in Gethsemane

Matthew 26:30-46; Mark 14:26-42; Luke 22:39-46

Jesus crossed over the brook Kidron into the Garden of Gethsemane
    Where He often went to pray. His disciples followed Him;
    He told them, "Sit here while I go elsewhere to pray."

Jesus took with Him Peter, James, and John. He said to them,
    "My soul is worried and sorrowful to death;
    "Watch and pray, I will go a little farther to pray."
Jesus bowed to the ground and prayed, "O Father if possible,
    I don't want to drink this cup of suffering. Let it pass Me by,
    Nevertheless, it's not what I want that matters; I will do Your
    will."
An angel was sent to strengthen Him, so Jesus
    Prayed more fervently with agony,
    And great drops of blood—as sweat—fell to the ground.
Jesus got up from His knees and came to the disciples
    But found them sleeping. He said to them,

"Could you not pray with Me one hour?"
Then Jesus challenged them, "Watch with Me in prayer,
    The Spirit is willing but the flesh is weak."
Jesus went back to pray a second time saying, "O Father,
    If this cup cannot pass away except I drink it,
    Then Your will be done."
Jesus came a second time to find His disciples sleeping
    Because they couldn't keep their eyes open;
    So He went back and prayed the same words a third time.
He said, "Sleep on, you need your rest";
    The hour is now that I'll be delivered to the betrayer."

Lord, forgive my prayerlessness; help me to be faithful in prayer
    Intercessing for the things You want done.

Jesus Betrayed, Arrested, and Forsaken

Matthew 26:47-56; Mark 14:43-52; Luke 22:47-53; John 18:2-12

Judas knew the place where Jesus often went to prayer
    So he led Roman soldiers and officers from the religious leaders
    With lanterns, torches and weapons to arrest Jesus.
Jesus knew what was happening so He met them and asked,
    "Who are you looking for?" They answered, "Jesus of Nazareth."
Jesus responded, "I am He," His statement of deity;
    Then the Roman soldiers and Jewish guards
    Were driven backward to the ground.
Again Jesus asked, "Who are you looking for?"
    They said, "Jesus of Nazareth."
Jesus answered, "I told you, I am He." Since you want Me,
    Let these go." Thus prophecy was fulfilled,
    "I lost none of those that You gave Me."
Judas had given them a sign that Jesus would be the one whom he kissed;

"Arrest Him!" So Judas kissed Jesus, and the Master answered,
  "Are you betraying the Son of Man with a kiss?"
As the guards moved forward to take Jesus, Simon Peter, having a sword,
  Cut off the right ear of Malchus, the High Priest's servant.
Jesus answered, "Put up your sword, I must drink the cup of suffering
  The Father has for Me"; then Jesus touched him and healed him.
They grabbed Jesus and bound Him, but He responded,
  "Have you come out in the middle of the night to arrest a thief?
"I sat daily in the temple, but you didn't arrest Me,"
  But this came to pass because it was predicted in Scripture;
  Then the disciples left Jesus and fled into the night.

Lord, may I always stand courageously for You
  And not run away as the disciples.

Chapter 16

JESUS' LAST DAYS ON EARTH

The Story of Jesus' Arrest and Interrogation

The tramp of Roman troops echoed through the streets of Jerusalem in the early morning hours of Friday, just after midnight. Levitical guards from the temple followed after the soldiers.

Annas was the power behind the office of the high priest, even though Rome had removed him from office because he would not fully cooperate with them. In Annas' place, Rome had appointed his son-in-law, Caiaphas. But the Jews still considered Annas God's instrument.

Dawn was coming, and Annas and the priests needed to agree on a legal charge that would be lodged against Jesus. Because the Romans did not allow Jewish officials to exercise capital punishment, only the Romans could execute Jesus. Therefore, the charge must be worthy of swift execution. But when Annas interrogated Jesus regarding His teachings, Jesus would not answer his questions.

"I have spoken openly to the world," Jesus replied. "Ask those who heard Me. Surely they know what I said."

When Jesus said this, one of the temple guards struck Him in the face. "Is this the way You answer a high priest?"

"If I have said something evil," Jesus said, "then tell Me what evil I have spoken. But if I spoke the truth, then why do you strike Me?"

Annas had heard enough. Any official charges would have to be made by his son-in-law Caiaphas and the Sanhedrin anyway, so Annas sent Jesus to Caiaphas' palace.

As the temple guard led Jesus, bound, toward Caiaphas' quarters, Peter and the youngest apostle John fell in behind the procession. At Caiaphas' house, the temple guard entered with Jesus, but the woman at the door kept the others out.

John recognized the girl and approached her, saying, "You know me. My father is Zebedee who sells fish to Caiaphas." She allowed John to enter the courtyard, while Peter waited outside.

Caiaphas was jittery, high-strung, explosive. As Jesus was brought in, the high priest babbled, "I have You now, Galilean! Your fate is in my hands."

But although Caiaphas wanted to summarily order an execution, Rome had taken the death penalty from the Jews. He could excommunicate Jesus, but what good was that? He would gladly kill Jesus with his bare hands, but his position wouldn't allow him.

John got Peter into the courtyard; Peter gravitated toward the red glow of a charcoal fire. Several bearded men huddled around it to warm their faces. Peter attempted to blend in with the men, appearing to be indifferent to what was going on. Then he was spotted by the young woman at the door. "You were with Jesus of Nazareth, the man they have on trial upstairs."

"Not me," Peter protested. "I don't know Him."

Confusion reigned upstairs in the palace. Dawn was rapidly approaching, and those gathered in the second-floor chamber couldn't agree on a charge to bring against Jesus.

Proof was needed if any charge was to hold water with the Roman governor, Pontius Pilate. Many council members knew someone who could bring charges against Jesus, some of whom would accept payment to make false accusations. Quickly, servants were dispatched to find those witnesses.

Members of the Sanhedrin tried to coerce their servants to give testimony. But it didn't work. First one man would speak out against Jesus, then another would contradict his story.

Jesus stood in silence. Caiaphas fidgeted in his seat.

Since the servants and false witnesses could not get their stories straight, some of the members of the Sanhedrin brought charges against Jesus. One of the council members stepped forward, charging, "This fellow said that He was able to destroy the temple and build it again within three days."

Nervous laughter filled the room. They all had heard about this claim.

"His violent hands have been raised against the temple of God!" the council member continued.

Caiaphas seized the opportunity to cross-examine Jesus. "What do You say to this charge?"

When Jesus did not answer, Caiaphas demanded: "Tell me who You are!"

Jesus answered, "Ask your witnesses. They know what I said."

Caiaphas jumped to his feet, waving frantically. "I demand by the Living God: Tell us whether You are the Christ, the Son of God!"

As the echoes died, Jesus responded, "Yes, it is as you say. One day you will see the Son of Man sitting at the right hand of the Mighty One on the clouds of Heaven."

"Blasphemy!" the high priest cried. "This is blasphemy!" The Sanhedrin knew the law, that if one were pronounced guilty he could be tried on the same day, but not punished on that same day. However, in the case of blasphemy, the offender could be judged immediately.

"Put Him to death!" the high priest screamed at the top of his voice. "We'll charge Him with blasphemy before Pilate."

The crowd muttered their agreement, and Caiaphas asked, "What think you, gentlemen? For life?"

Silence.

"For death?"

"For death!" the priests cried.

"Then we shall recommend this sentence to our friend Pilate." Peter sat by the wall, despairing. He had heard the cry "For death!" from the upper chamber.

Then out of the darkness stepped a temple guard, a cousin to Malchus, the young priest whose ear Peter had cut off. He challenged Peter. "Didn't I see you with Jesus in the olive grove?"

"You are mistaken, sir," Peter said nervously. "I do not know the man."

Within the same hour, another guard stood with Peter by the fire, saying to his comrades, "Certainly this fellow was with him, for he is a Galilean." Then he said to Peter, "You are a Galilean. Your accent gives you away!"

"I tell you, I do not know the man!" Peter blurted out. He vowed an oath to God that he did not know Jesus.

At that moment, Jesus was led down the stairs and into the courtyard. Jesus glanced over at Peter, and their eyes met. Even before the tears came to Peter's eyes, a heaving sob welled up within him. He rushed out the front gate and into the darkness.

In the distance, a rooster crowed.

The First Trial—Before Annas, the Former High Priest

John 18:12-24

The soldiers and guards led Jesus bound to Annas
      The former High Priest who was deposed for his corruption
      And put Caiaphas his son-in-law into that office.
Annas asked Jesus about His disciples and what He taught;
      Jesus answered, "I spoke openly in synagogues and

The temple and I kept back nothing secretly.
"Ask those who heard Me what I taught";
    When Jesus answered this way, an officer struck Jesus
    With his hand saying, "Why do You answer the High Priest so?"
Jesus replied, "Tell me if I have spoken evil;
    If not, then don't strike Me."

Lord, thank You for being faithful at Your trial;
    Though You never sinned, you died for my sin.

The Second Trial—Before Caiaphas

Matthew 26:57-68; Mark 14:53-65; Luke 22:54-65; John 18:15-27

Annas sent Jesus bound to Caiaphas to determine the indictment;
    Simon Peter and John followed Jesus, only John was known
    By the gate keeper so he entered the compound, but not Peter.
John spoke to the maid and she let Peter into the yard;
    She said to Peter, "You're a disciple of Jesus";
    Peter answered, "I am not"!
The servants were warming themselves at a fire
    For it was cold and Peter also warmed himself.
The religious leaders had gotten false witnesses against Jesus
    Because they had agreed Jesus must die.
But the false witnesses didn't agree. One witness said,
    "I heard Jesus say He would destroy the temple
    And rebuild it in three days without hands."
The High Priest asked Jesus why He didn't answer them,
    But Jesus held His peace and didn't answer them.
The High Priest then demanded, "Tell us if you're
    The Messiah, the Son of the Blessed."
Jesus answered, "I am, and you shall see the Son of Man
    Sitting next to the Father, when He'll come

With the clouds of Heaven."
The High Priest ripped his official robe in disgust saying,
    "We don't need witnesses, He has spoken blasphemy";
    The crowd shouted, "He is worthy of death"!
Then they spit in His face and slapped Him around;
    They covered His eyes and said, "Prophesy...who hit You?"

Peter was standing to warm himself when one asked,
    "Are you one of Jesus' disciples?"
    Peter answered, "I am not!"
One of the servants of the High Priest—a relative of the one whose ear
    Peter cut off—also said, "Didn't I see you in the garden with
    Jesus"?
Peter cursed and said, "I swear, I don't know Him";
    Knowing all things, Jesus turned to look out the
    Window at Peter and Peter saw his Lord looking at him.
The rooster crowed and Peter remembered what Jesus said,
    And he left the house and wept bitterly.

Lord, help me to be faithful to You and never deny You
    As Peter denied You.

The Third Trial—Before the Sanhedrin

Matthew 27:1; Mark 15:1; Luke 22:66-71

As soon as it was day, the Sanhedrin assembled
    At the directives of the High Priest who led Jesus there.
They asked, "Tell us if You are the Messiah-Deliver;
    Jesus answered, "You won't believe if I tell you
    But you will see Me seated at the right hand of God."
Then they asked, "Are You the Son of God?"
    Jesus answered, "I am what you ask."

Then the council concluded, "We don't need witnesses,
  He is guilty of blasphemy as we thought."

Lord, even though the elected leaders spoke for all Israel
when they rejected Jesus,
  I have received Him and will follow Him.

The Story of Judas' Suicide

The well-dressed man was frantic. He pushed his way through the crowd streaming out of the temple.

"I have sinned…," Judas panted in a low voice. "Get out of my way!"

I have sinned! he thought. *I must see the priests now!*

One of the priests recognized Judas and opened a side door to him. Judas fought his way in and ran toward the caucus room where he had made his deal with the enemies of Jesus. He came face to face with a knot of laughing priests.

"You must stop this execution!" Judas demanded.

But they laughed all the harder. "You have your money. Take your silver and go."

But Judas had to cleanse his soul. With a hoarse cry, he sobbed, "I have sinned…I am doomed to hell!"

The priests laughed. They had no words of mercy for Judas. Judas glared wildly, his chest heaving with anger and sorrow. Then he untied the bag holding the 30 pieces of silver, removed a coin and turned it over in his hand. He ran out the door toward the sanctuary of the temple.

"Wait!" the priests shouted. They could not allow him to do what it appeared he might do.

Judas ran wildly toward the Court of Israel. It was there that penitent worshipers would wait while the priests offered sacrifice of forgiveness for them. With a mad cry, he hurled the 30 pieces of silver onto the marble pavement, yelling, "I have sinned! I need forgiveness!"

Before the priests could reach him, Judas fled the temple and ran down into the valley.

Judas crossed the valley, frantically climbing up the steep ascent to the place called Potter's Field. Around its edge, cliffs dropped into the valley. The cliffs were lined with jagged rocks.

Judas was heading to a gnarled tree that grew there—a tree that extended from the cliff out over the valley. There Judas knelt to untie his sash.

For the past day, his mind had been in a storm. Now he grew calm. He had returned the silver and had asked for forgiveness. He couldn't believe it was forthcoming, however, and he knew what he must do.

Judas tied one end of the sash around his neck. Then he climbed the tree, leaning out over the precipice to attach the sash to the tree limb. The tree was visible across the Hinnom Valley, so those in the city would be able to see what he was about to do. Judas wanted his death to send a message.

Returning to the ground, Judas was ready. He stood at the edge of the cliff, looking across the valley to Jerusalem.

Then Judas jumped out over the precipice. He swung for a moment, but the knot in his sash loosened under his weight. Judas fell onto the jagged rocks beneath. His intestines spilled out as the body bounced to the bottom of the gorge.

Remorse and Suicide of Judas

Matthew 27:3-10; Acts 1:18,19

Judas was guilty because he betrayed Jesus;
>He repented and brought the 30 pieces of silver
>Back to the religious rulers saying,

"I have sinned because I betrayed an innocent man."
The religious rulers laughed at him saying, "We don't care";
    Judas threw the 30 pieces on the sanctuary floor
    And went to the land that he bought with
    The money he stole from the bag.
Judas hanged himself out over a cliff, but the
    Knot broke and he fell into a ravine;
    His intestines burst out and he died.
The religious leaders would not accept the 30 pieces
    Because it was blood money so they
    Bought a burial ground for the poor who
    Can't afford a grave, thus fulfilling the
    Prophecy of Jeremiah (Jer. 18:2; 19:2; 32:6-15).

The Fourth Trial—Before Pilate

Matthew 27:11-14; Mark 15:1-5; Luke 23:1-7; John 18:19-38

And they bound Jesus again and led Him to Pilate's palace
    After the sun was up, but the Jewish leaders wouldn't enter
    Because they didn't want to defile themselves for the Passover.
Pilate went out to them and asked, "What is the legal indictment?"
    They answered, "If this man were not guilty,
    We wouldn't have brought Him to you."
Pilate said, "Then judge Him according to your law";
    They answered, "We do not have the authority to execute anyone."
The religious rulers said Jesus was against paying taxes to Caesar
    And called Him the Messiah-King.
Pilate went inside to Jesus and asked Him, "Are You the King of the
    Jews?" Jesus answered, "Did you think up this question, or
    Did someone plant it in your mind?"
Pilate answered, "I am not a Jew. Your religious leaders

Brought You to me; what have You done?"
Jesus answered, "My Kingdom is not of this world. If it were,
My followers would fight to rescue Me. Since they
Haven't come for Me, then My Kingdom is different."
Pilate answered, "Then You are a King!"
Jesus replied, "You said it. That's the reason
I was born that I should reveal this truth
And everyone who follows truth, would follow Me."
Pilate questioned, "What is truth?" He didn't wait for an answer
But went out to the Jewish leaders and concluded,
"I find no crime in this man!"

Lord, even though Pilate rejected the kingship of Jesus,
I crown Him as King of my life and obey Him.

The Fifth Trial of Jesus

Luke 23:6-12

When Pilate heard the continuous yelling of the Jewish leaders,
He asked if Jesus were a Galilean.
So then Pilate sent Jesus to King Herod who was over Galilee;
Herod was in Jerusalem for the Passover.
Herod was glad to see Jesus because of the Miracle-worker's reputation;
Herod wanted to see Jesus perform a miracle.
The Galilean king asked questions
But Jesus didn't answer any of them.
The religious leaders kept repeating their accusations against Jesus,
So Herod mocked Jesus and dressed Him in kingly apparel
And sent Jesus back to Pilate.
Herod and Pilate became friends that day, previously they were
Political rivals and hated each other.

Lord, it's amazing how hatred for Jesus brings enemies together,
   And how love for Jesus brings me closer to
   Others who also love Him.

The Sixth Trial of Jesus

Matthew 27:15-26; Mark 15:6-15; Luke 23:13-25; John 18:39–19:16

Pilate was reluctant to give in to the demands of the religious leaders
   So he planned to release a criminal which was the custom at
   Passover.
Pilate asked, "Should I release the King of the Jews, or should I release
   Barabbas who is a lawless man and a murderer?"
The religious leaders stirred up the crowd to demand Barabbas' release
   So Pilate asked, "What shall I do with the one called 'King of
   the Jews?'"
   The crowd yelled "Crucify Him."
Pilate answered, "What evil has Jesus done?
   I find no cause to execute Him."
The crowd yelled louder, "Crucify Him!"
   Pilate was afraid of the consequences, so he re-entered
   The palace and said to Jesus, "Who are You?"
   But Jesus didn't answer Him.
Pilate rebuked Jesus, "Why are You silent? I have the authority to
   Release You or to crucify You."
Jesus said, "You have no authority that's not given to you from above;
   The Jews who brought Me to you have the greater sin."
Pilate made plans to release Jesus, but the Jews cried even louder,
   "Crucify Him. If you release Him you are not Caesar's friend;
   Everyone who calls Himself a king is Caesar's enemy."

Lord, I like that Barabbas goes free while Jesus is crucified in my place.
   Thank You for dying for me.

The Story of Jesus Being Whipped

Jesus was dragged into the belly of Antonia. The Roman guards hooked the thongs binding His wrists to a beating post, extending His arms above his head. They ripped His tunic to the waist, and the olive skin of His back was revealed.

A soldier took hold of a cat-o'-nine-tails, a leather whip of nine thongs.

"ONE!" A centurion yelled out as the guard laid the first stripes on Jesus' back. But there was no sound from Jesus.

"TWO!" came the second command. No sound from Jesus.

"THREE!" Still no sound from Jesus.

The lashes reached 39. "If He dies with 39 stripes," was the common refrain, "then it proves He was guilty." But the scourging didn't kill Jesus. It merely humiliated and tortured Him.

The soldiers loosed the knot in the straps about His wrists, and Jesus crumbled in a heap. One of the soldiers draped a scarlet robe across His swollen back. Then they twisted together a crown of thorns and set it on His head. They placed a reed in His right hand, pretending it was a royal scepter. Then, bowing before Him in mockery, one of the soldiers said, "Hail, king of the Jews," and the others laughed.

Dragging Jesus up the stairs into the judgment hall, the soldiers threw Him onto the floor before Pilate. Rising from his breakfast, Pilate walked around Jesus, who was a pitiful sight.

Perhaps, Pilate thought, the indignities this man had suffered would appease the priests. So he took Jesus by the arm and drew Him to the porch.

"*Behold the man*," Pilate called for all to hear. "I have brought Him out to show you what you have done and to let you know once more that I find no basis for a charge against Him."

And the chief priests and Pharisees took up the shout once more: "Crucify Him! Nail Him to the cross!"

Pilate said to them, "You crucify Him! I find no fault in Him." The Jewish leaders had not expected the Roman governor to be so squeamish. Frustrated, the priests announced, "We have a law, and according to that law He must die, because He claimed to be the Son of God."

But this did not move Pilate. Jesus had not broken any Roman law, only their Jewish traditions. Pilate pondered his dilemma. He took Jesus inside and demanded of Him, "Don't you realize I have the power either to free You or to crucify You?" Then Jesus answered him, saying, "You would have no power over Me if it were not given to you from above."

When Pilate returned to the porch, the spokesman for the chief priests shouted, "If you let this man go, you are no friend of Caesar. Anyone who claims to be a king opposes Caesar. Jesus of Nazareth has set himself to be king, and that is treason!" Pilate could not ignore this line of reasoning.

"Shall I then crucify your king?" Pilate cried out to the leaders.

"We have no king but Caesar," they answered.

Pilate knew the Jews' long-standing hatred of Roman rule. Their hatred for this Galilean must run even deeper. He handed Jesus over to be crucified.

Jesus is Mocked

Matthew 27:27-34; Mark 15:16-23; Luke 23:26-36; John 19:17-29

Pilate released Barabbas, but he had Jesus scourged;
    The soldiers then led Jesus to the dungeon
      Where they stripped Him and beat Him mercilessly.
The soldiers mocked Jesus and put a purple robe on Him
    And made a crown of thorns and jammed it on His head;
      They put a stick in His right hand and bowed in mock worship
    Saying, "Hail, King of the Jews."
Then the soldiers took the stick and beat Him on the head,
    And spit on Him.

Finally, the soldiers took the purple robe off Him
    And put His robe back on Jesus
    And led Him back to Pilate.

Lord, I was "In Christ" when He suffered for me,
    I will always be grateful that He was punished in my place.

So Pilate had Jesus brought out and placed on the judgment tribunal
    And pronounced, "Behold Your King;
    It was six o'clock in the morning
    When the Passover Lamb was sacrificed.

Lord, I accepted Jesus when He was presented to me,
    I did not reject Him as did the Jews.

The crowd seeing Jesus cried again, "Crucify Him."
    Pilate answered, "Shall I crucify your King?"
    The crowd answered, "We have no king but Caesar."
Then Pilate took water and washed his hands saying, "I am
    Innocent of the blood of this righteous man."
    The Jews said, "His blood be on us and our children."
The soldiers then led Jesus away to be crucified;
    They made Jesus carry His cross to Calvary.

Jesus was exhausted and weakened so He fell under the load of the cross,
    The soldiers made Simeon from North Africa carry the cross.
A large crowd followed Jesus, including many weeping women
    But Jesus told them, "Daughters of Jerusalem, don't weep for Me,
    But shed your tears for yourselves and your children;
For there is coming tribulation when people will pray
    For the mountains to fall on them."

Lord, the Jews have suffered because they rejected their Messiah-Deliver;
    I have accepted Jesus and He has blessed my life.

Jesus' Last Days on Earth

And when they came to Golgotha—the place of a skull—
>They offered Him wine as an anesthesia to block the pain,
>But Jesus would not drink it.

The Story of Jesus on the Cross

The scarlet robe was torn off Jesus' body, causing His wounds to bleed afresh. He was led out of the fortress toward the hill called Golgotha—Calvary in Greek—which means the Place of the Skull.

A centurion led a detachment of four men, a hammer swinging menacingly from his belt. The soldiers made sure the victim carried His own instrument of execution—a wooden cross. But after the scourging, Jesus was too weak to carry His load. He continually fell. "Up!" one of the soldiers cried again and again, each time beating Jesus with a rope.

Behind Jesus came two thieves, each carrying his own cross. Following close behind was John, the only apostle who hadn't run away.

Word of these happenings had reached many who believed Jesus' teaching. Hundreds of weeping men and women now lined the street, mingling with His detractors.

A wooden shingle was placed around Jesus' neck; later it would be nailed to the top of the cross. On the shingle Pilate had written, "JESUS OF NAZARETH, THE KING OF THE JEWS."

After Jesus had fallen several times along the route, the Roman soldiers didn't waste time beating Him again.

"You!" the centurion yelled to a man in the crowd.

Simon, a pilgrim from the land of Cyrene, was dressed differently; his dark-green robe and red tunic stood out in the crowd of white and brown tunics. "Pick up that cross and follow us."

So Simon the Cyrenian hefted the cross onto his shoulder and carried it for Jesus to the place called Golgotha.

283

The heavy timbers made a cracking sound as Simon dropped the cross at the top of the hill. Calloused hands stripped the sandals, cloak, and tunic from Jesus and stretched Him on the timbers. Ropes tied His hands and feet to the cross. Then a Roman soldier, swinging a large wooden mallet, approached Jesus. This muscular man took a black iron spike, placed it in the palm of Jesus' right hand and with a mighty swing of his hammer, began driving the spike into the timber.

THWAPPP..., the sound rang out. THWAPPP...THWAPPP... The soldiers didn't pay any attention—they had heard the sound many times.

Next, the executioner turned to Jesus' other hand, repeating the process. He lifted the hammer. THWAPPP...THWAPPP...THWAPPP...

He did the same to the feet of Jesus.

A hole almost two feet deep had been chiseled out of the limestone. With Jesus nailed to the cross, the soldiers put their huge shoulders to the weight. Slowly they lifted the cross skyward. The weight of Jesus' body caused the nails in His hands and feet to rip His flesh. His body screamed in agony, but he said nothing. The soldiers raised the cross until it was nearly upright. Then the executioner kicked it so that the base of the cross dropped into the hole.

THUMP...Jesus shut His eyes as His body shook with pain, but He said nothing for a moment. Then He lifted His eyes to Heaven in prayer, "Father, forgive them, for they know not what they do." It was nine o'clock in the morning.

On the Cross
9 A.M. to 12 Noon

Matthew 27:35-44; Mark 15:24-32; Luke 23:33-43; John 19:18-27

They nailed Jesus to the cross and lifted it up
    Then they crucified two thieves, one on each side of Jesus.
The four soldiers divided His possessions, each one taking a fourth;

Because His robe didn't have a seam, they didn't rip it up
But cast dice for it, thus fulfilling Scripture.
"They divided My clothes and cast lots for My robe" (Ps. 22:18).

Jesus' First Statement From the Cross

Luke 23:34-42

And Jesus cried with a loud voice so everyone heard,
"Father, forgive them, they don't know what they've done."

Lord, thank You for forgiving me all my sins,
Especially when I didn't know what I was doing.

Pilate had written the indictment for which Jesus was executed
On a shingle and it was nailed on the cross over His head,
JESUS OF NAZARETH, KING OF THE JEWS.
The indictment was written in Latin, Greek, and Hebrew and
Everyone could read it from the nearby roadway.
The Jewish leaders asked Pilate to change the wording because
It embarrassed them. But Pilate answered,
"No, what I have written will remain on the cross."

Lord, even though Jesus died as the rejected King of Israel,
I recognize His authority and role in my life.

Then travelers on the road laughed at Jesus saying, "You claim
To destroy the temple in three days and rebuild it,
Why can't You come down from the cross?"
The religious leaders mocked Jesus saying, "You saved others,
Why can't You save Yourself?"
"If You are the Messiah-Deliverer, come down from Your cross
So we can see and believe in You";
Both thieves on either side also mocked Jesus.
One thief repeated the mockery, "If You are Messiah,

Save Yourself and us";
The other thief rebuked him saying, "We deserve to die
Because we are thieves, but this man doesn't deserve this."
Then he said, "Jesus, remember me when You
Come into Your Kingdom."

Jesus' Second Statement From the Cross

Luke 23:43

Jesus answered, "Today, you shall be with Me in paradise."

Lord, I'm glad You remembered me when You hung on the cross,
I will live with You forever because You forgave my sin.

John returned to the Cross with Mary, Jesus' mother,
And Mary the wife of Cleophus and Mary Magdalene.

Jesus' Third Statement From the Cross

John 19:25-27

When Jesus saw His mother, He said, "Woman, behold your son";
Then nodding to John—the disciple who loved Him—Jesus said,
"Son, behold your mother." They left as John took Mary
To his own home.

From Noon Until 3 P.M.

Matthew 27:45-50; Mark 15:33-37; Luke 23:44-46; John 19:28-30

When high noon came, darkness covered the land
Till 3 P.M. and the sunlight failed.

Jesus' Fourth Statement From the Cross

Matthew 27:45-49; Mark 15:33-36

Then Jesus cried with a loud voice, *Eli, Eli, toma sabachthani,*
"My God, My God, why have You forsaken Me?"
Some thought Jesus was calling for Elijah.

One ran to fill a sponge with vinegar and
Put it on a reed, then gave Him to drink saying,
"Let's see if Elijah comes to take Him down."

Jesus' Fifth Statement From the Cross

John 19:28

Jesus realized He was going to die, knowing all things
Were accomplished that were required for a substitutionary death,
Said, "I thirst."

Lord, I identify with the humanity of Jesus, and
I realize my limitations and my thirst,
Just as Jesus realized His physical need.

Jesus' Sixth Statement From the Cross

John 19:29-30

When Jesus received the vinegar, he again shouted,
"It is finished."

Lord, thank You that Jesus finished my salvation
And there is nothing left for Him to do
To save me from my sin.

Jesus' Seventh Statement From the Cross

Luke 23:46

When three o'clock came, Jesus again shouted,
    "Father, into Your hands I commend My Spirit."
Then Jesus in one final act of humanity, bowed His head
    And gave up the ghost. No one took His life from Him,
    He gave it freely for the world.

Lord, when it comes time for me to die,
    What else can I do but commend my Spirit to you,
    Then wait for You to receive me into Heaven.

The Accompanying Phenomena

Matthew 27:51-56; Mark 15:38-41; Luke 23:45-49

When the Centurion, who commanded the soldiers,
    Saw that Jesus gave up the ghost he said,
    "Truly, this man was the righteous Son of God."
The veil in the temple that concealed the Holy of Holies
    Was ripped from top to bottom.
An earthquake shook the area, and rocks tumbled to the ground
    And tore open the graves, then
    Many bodies of the Saints in the graves were raised.
They came out of the tombs after Jesus' resurrection
    And appeared to many who saw them.
There was a group of women watching from a distant hill
    Made up of Mary Magdalene; Mary, the mother of James the Less,
    And Joseph, the mother of James and John and Salome.
These were the women who followed Jesus in Galilee and paid for
    The expenses. They had followed Him to Jerusalem.

Lord, I was there when Jesus died, for I was
"In Christ," being baptized into His death;
I know my sins were forgiven when He died.

The Burial of Jesus' Body

Matthew 27:57-60; Mark 15:42-46; Luke 23:50-54; John 19:31-42

The Jewish leaders asked Pilate to take down the three bodies
>Because they didn't want them on the crosses on the Passover.

They asked Pilate to break their legs to kill them
>If they were not already dead.

When the soldiers came to Jesus, they didn't
>Break His legs because He was already dead,
>Fulfilling the Scripture, "Not a bone of Him was broken."

But a soldier pierced the side of Jesus with his spear;
>Immediately, blood and water came out of the wound.

John the apostle saw this happen and witnessed in
>His Gospel that these things happened, so that
>Readers may believe in Jesus and be saved.

Finally, the crowd that came to see the crucifixion
>Returned to the city in a somber mood, again fulfilling Scripture,
>"They looked on Him whom they pierced."

As the evening approached, Joseph of Arimathea,
>A member of the Sanhedrin, went to ask Pilate for the body of Jesus
>To give it a proper burial.

Pilate was surprised that Jesus was already dead,
>So he called the Centurion who supervised the crucifixion
>To verify that Jesus was actually dead.

When Pilate found out Jesus was in fact dead,
>He gave Joseph the authority to bury the body.

Joseph was a believer who looked for the coming Kingdom,
    Who was a member of the Sanhedrin,
    But he was not there to vote for the death of Jesus.
Nicodemus joined him, who also was a member of the Sanhedrin,
    And a secret believer in Jesus Christ,
    But for fear of the Jews didn't tell anyone.
Joseph took the body down from the cross, and wrapped it
    In clean linen cloths and anointed it
    With 75 pounds of myrrh and aloes which was Jewish custom.
Near Golgotha was a garden in which was located
    A tomb where no one had been buried.
It had been newly carved out of rock
    And was intended to bury Joseph of Arimathea.
They buried Jesus just as the Jewish ritual demanded
    Because the Passover was celebrated at sundown.

Lord, I was buried with Jesus because the Bible says,
    "Buried with Him by baptism unto death,
    To be raised to newness of life."

Friday Until Sunday Morning

Matthew 27:61-66; Mark 15:47; Luke 23:55-56

The women continued their watch from a distance,
    Mary Magdalene, Mary the mother of Joseph,
    And the other women who followed Jesus from Galilee.
On Saturday, the religious leaders went to see Pilate
    Saying, "When the deceiver was alive, He
    Claimed He would rise from the dead on the third day."
So they asked Pilate to secure the grave with
    Soldiers until after the third day to make sure
    The disciples didn't come steal the body and claim,
"He is risen from the dead, and the last error becomes

Greater than the first."
Pilate said, "Take guards and go make the grave
As secure as you are able to do."
So they took guards and a Roman seal secured
The tomb.

Lord, the world will do anything to deny Your resurrection,
But I know You were raised from the dead,
Because You live within my heart.

Chapter 17

THE RESURRECTION OF JESUS CHRIST

At the Tomb Early Sunday Morning

Matthew 28:2-4;11-15

Behold there was a great earthquake when the angel of the Lord

    Descended from Heaven to roll away the stone

    From the grave and he sat on it.

He was bright as lightning and his clothes were

    As white as snow. The guards fainted dead away.

Some of the guards went into the city and told the religious leaders

    What happened at the tomb.

The Sanhedrin assembled to discuss the matter, then they

    Gave money to the soldiers to bribe them to say,

    "The disciples came while we slept and stole His body."

The religious leaders told the soldiers if this gets

    To your superiors, we will persuade them to

    Look the other way.

The soldiers took the money and did as they were told,

    So the rumor spread throughout the city that

    The disciples stole the body. The Jews believed

    This explanation until this day.

The Visit of the Women to the Tomb

Matthew 28:1-8; Mark 16:1-8; Luke 24:1-8; John 20:1

Early on Sunday morning, Mary Magdalene, Mary the
    Mother of James, Salome and the other women,
    Went to the tomb before the sun came up.
They said among themselves, "Who will roll away the stone?"
    They brought spices to anoint the body of Jesus.
Because Mary Magdalene was more courageous, she left them
    And went ahead to spy at the soldiers' camp.
When she saw the stone rolled from the tomb,
    She left and ran to tell Peter and John;
    She didn't return to the women she left behind.
She told the two disciples, "They have taken away the Lord
    Out of the tomb, and I don't know where He is."

Lord, I admire the ignorant zeal of Mary Magdalene;,
    May I always serve You zealously
    Whether I know or don't know what I'm doing.

The other women were concerned when Mary didn't return,
    They went to the tomb and saw the stone rolled away.
They entered the tomb and were shocked to see a young man
    Sitting there in a dazzling white robe.
He said, "Don't be shocked, you seek Jesus of Nazareth;
    He is risen. Look at the place where they laid Him.
"Go tell His disciples and Peter, He will go before
    You to Galilee."
The women were overjoyed, so they ran to
    Tell His disciples, but Jesus met them in the way;
    They held Jesus by the feet, worshiping Him.
Jesus told them, "Don't fear, tell My followers to go
    To Galilee where they will see Me."

Peter and John Visit the Tomb

John 20:2-10

On a separate road, Peter and John ran to the tomb;
    The younger John outran Peter.
John looked inside the tomb and saw the linen clothes
    Still wrapped together, but he didn't go in.

Peter didn't stop, but ran straight into the tomb
    And also saw the linen clothes together and the death mask
    Lying at another place.
Next, John entered the tomb—examined everything—then
    He believed that Jesus had risen from the dead;
    They returned to their house.

Lord, I believe You arose physically from the dead,
    I don't need the proof of an empty tomb
    Because I have You in my heart.

Mary Returns to the Tomb

John 20:11-18

Later that morning, Mary Magdalene returned to the tomb,
    She wept as she looked into the tomb.
Then she saw two angels—clothed in white—sitting
    At the head and feet where the body had been laid.
"Woman, why are you crying," the angels asked.
    She answered, "Because they have taken away
    My Lord and I don't know where He is located."
Someone was standing back of her, but she didn't
    Know who it was. She thought he was a gardener
    So she asked,
"If you have taken away His body, tell me where it is

And I will take Him away."
It was Jesus who said, "Mary." Her blindness
Was taken away and she called Him, "Rabboni,"
An old Hebrew word for "respected master."
Jesus said, "Quit clinging to Me as though things
Will continue in the future as they were in the past."
Jesus explained, "I must go to My Father in Heaven,
He is also your Father. He is My God and your God."
Mary returned to Jerusalem to tell the brethren,
"I have seen the Lord." Then she told them
All the things Jesus said to her.

Lord, may I be a witness to You of all I've experienced.
Use me to tell others of Your death and resurrection.

Jesus Appears on the Road to Emmaus

Luke 24:13-32

Sunday afternoon, Cleophus and his wife were walking
Home from Jerusalem, talking about all the things
That happened over the weekend.
Jesus joined them but they didn't know it was Jesus;
He said to them, because they looked so sad,
"What are you talking about?"
They answered, "Are You the only one in Jerusalem
Who doesn't know what happened this weekend?"
Jesus answered, "What things?" They answered,
"The things that happened to Jesus of Nazareth."
They explained Jesus was a prophet who did mighty miracles
But the religious leaders delivered Him to Pilate
Who condemned Him to death and crucified Him.
The couple said, "We hoped He would have delivered Israel
But today—the third day—some women went

To the tomb early and found it empty.
"Then the women claimed to have seen angels, and
That Jesus was alive.
"Some men also went to the tomb and found it empty, as
The women said, but they didn't see Him."
Then Jesus said, "You are foolish not to believe all
The prophets have predicted. They said the Messiah
Must suffer before entering His glory."
Jesus began at the books of Moses and covered the Scriptures
To the prophets, explaining to them
All the Scriptures said about Himself.
As they drew near their home in Emmaus, Jesus
Pretended He was going farther.
They invited Him into their home saying, "Abide
With us, because it is toward the evening."
Jesus went into the house with them and as they
Sat down to eat, Jesus took bread and blessed it
And gave it to them to eat.
Their eyes were opened and He vanished out of their sight;
They said to each other, "Didn't our hearts burn
Within us as He explained to us the Scriptures?"
Immediately, they returned to Jerusalem and found the disciples
Gathered together, and told them, "The Lord
Has arisen indeed and has appeared to us."
They rehearsed the things that happened that day,
Including the fact the Lord had appeared to Peter.

The Upper Room on Sunday Evening

Luke 24:36,37; John 20:19-25

When the evening came, ten disciples gathered in the Upper Room,
The doors were locked for fear of the Jews;

Jesus came to stand among them, and said, "Peace to you."
Jesus said, "Why are you afraid, and why are you
    So confused over what has happened?"
Jesus showed them His hands and feet, then said,
    "Handle Me, a Spirit doesn't have flesh
    And bones like this."
They were deliriously happy, yet still they had
    A hard time believing what they were seeing.
Jesus said, "What do you have to eat?" They gave
    Him some broiled fish and He ate it before them.

Lord, I believe You are totally human,
    But I also believe You are totally divine.

The disciples were glad to see and experience the presence
    Of the Lord. Then Jesus said again, "Peace to you.
    As the Father has sent Me into the world,
    So, I am sending you into the world."
Jesus breathed on them and said, "Receive the Holy Spirit
    To teach you and use you, just as He has done
Throughout the past dispensation. He will be
    With you until you are endued with His power."
"Those you lead to faith will have their sins forgiven,
    Those who reject will retain their sins."

Lord, I need the ministry of the Holy Spirit in all I do,
    I cannot serve You without His enablement;
    I yield to You, come fill me now.

Thomas, the disciple called Didymas—a twin—was not there;
    The disciples told him, "We have seen the Lord."
He said, "I must see the nail prints in His hands, and
    Put my hand into the wound in His side;
    Otherwise, I will not believe."

Lord, I'll not demand physical assurances to believe,
I believe You are the crucified Son of God who died for me.

The Upper Room One Week Later

Mark 16:14-18; John 20:26-31

Eight days after Passover, the disciples gathered again
    In the Upper Room on a Sunday evening;
    Thomas was with them this time.
The doors were locked but Jesus again stood among them
    And said what He said last Sunday, "Peace to you."
Jesus spoke first to Thomas, "Reach your finger to touch
    My wounds and place your hand in the wound
    In My side. Don't doubt, but believe."
But Thomas didn't do it, he answered, "You are my Lord
    And my God."
Jesus said, "God will bless you because you have
    Seen Me and believed. But God will also bless
    Those who haven't seen Me, yet they believe."
Jesus did many miracles that were not written in the Gospels,
    But these miracles are written that people will believe
    That Jesus is the Messiah, the Son of God.

I will believe that Jesus is the Son of God,
    And when I believe, I'll have eternal life.

Then Jesus repeated to them the commission,
    "Go into all the world and preach the Gospel to every person;
    Baptize those who believe, and those who won't believe
    Will be condemned."

"You will do miracles, speak in tongues, miraculously survive
Poisonous snake bites, and when men try to poison you;
You shall lay hands on the sick and they'll recover."

Jesus Appears on the Lake Shore

John 21

A week later, Jesus appeared to seven disciples
    On the shore of the Sea of Galilee.
Simon Peter had announced, "I am going fishing";
    There went with him Thomas, Nathaniel, James
    And John, Andrew, and Phillip.
They got into a boat and fished all night, but caught nothing;
    When the day was breaking, Jesus stood on the beach,
    But the disciples didn't know it was Jesus.
Jesus yelled to them, "Have you caught any fish?"
    They answered Him, "No!" Jesus answered, "Cast the net
    On the other side of the boat and you will catch fish."
They cast on the right side and couldn't draw in the fish,
    So John said to Peter, "It's the Lord."
Peter put on his tunic and dove into the water
    To swim to Jesus. The other disciples came in a
    Little boat, for they were 100 yards from the beach.
When they got to shore, they saw a charcoal fire cooking fish,
    There was also bread;
    Jesus said, "Add the fish you've caught to these."
Simon Peter went and pulled the net to land, it had 153 fish
    In it, yet the net didn't break.
Jesus said, "Come eat, break your fast." No one asked
    Who it was, for they all knew it was Jesus;
    Jesus served all of them breakfast.
This was the third Sunday that Jesus appeared to them.

Lord, I can't see You physically, yet I see
    You in the pages of Scripture.

After breakfast, Jesus said, "Simon, Son of Jonah,
    Do you love Me more deeply than you love these nets?"

Peter answered, "Lord, You know that I like and admire You."

    Jesus answered, "Feed My lambs."

Jesus said to him a second time, "Simon, do you

    Deeply love Me?" Peter answered, "Lord, You know

    That I like and admire You." Jesus answered, "Tend My sheep."

Jesus said a third time, "Simon, do you really

    Like and admire Me?" Peter was ashamed the Lord

    Asked him three times, because he denied the Lord

    Three times, and because he only said he liked and admired the

    Lord.

So Peter answered, "Lord, You omnisciently know everything,

    You know I can only say I really like and admire You."

    Jesus said, "Feed My sheep."

Then Jesus predicted, "When you were young,

    You were able to dress yourself, and go where you wanted."

"But when you get old, they will stretch your hands

    Out on a cross and they will clothe you with

    What they choose, and lead you where they want to go."

This spoke Jesus indicating Peter would die as a martyr;

    Then Jesus concluded, "Follow Me."

Peter turned to John and asked Jesus, "What about him?"

    Jesus said, "If he lives till I return, how does

    That concern you? You must follow Me."

This statement made many think John would live until

    Jesus' return. But Jesus didn't say John wouldn't die,

    Only, "If he lives till I return, how does that concern you?"

Jesus did many other things; if they were all written

    The world couldn't contain the books that could be written.

Lord, I really love You with all my heart,

    Give me courage to tell everyone of my devotion to You.

The Appearance on a Mountain

Matthew 28:16-20; 1 Corinthians 15:6,7

On the fourth Sunday, Jesus appeared to approximately 500 people,
>Many were still alive when Paul wrote the letter to the Corinthians.
They worshiped when they saw Him, but some still doubted.
>Jesus said, "All authority in Heaven is given to Me,
>Go make disciples of all people groups in the world,
>Baptizing them in the name of the Father, Son, and Holy Spirit,
>Teaching them to obey all I command you.
>"And lo, I will be with you everywhere you go,
>Even to the ends of this age."

Lord, you've given the Great Commission to the church generally,
>*And to me specifically.*
>*Help me do my part to obey Your command.*

Jesus appears to His half-brother James
>Who was to become the leader of the church in Jerusalem,
>And He appeared privately to Peter.

Lord, I don't expect to see an appearance of You in the flesh,
>*But I know You are real because You live in my heart*
>*And that is just as real as if I saw you physically.*

Jesus' Appearance on the Fifth Sunday
And His Ascension Back to Heaven

Luke 24:44-53; Acts 1:3-12

Jesus appeared to His disciples in the city of Jerusalem
>On the fifth Sunday after His resurrection.
He said, "Remember the things I said before I died,
>That the things of Calvary must be completed because

They were predicted in Moses, the prophets, and the Psalms.
Then Jesus opened their spiritual eyes to understand these things,
Jesus said, "This is the Gospel that the Christ should suffer for
sins,
Be raised from the dead on the third day,
And that repentance and remission of sins be preached
In My name, in all the world, beginning at Jerusalem.
"You will have everything the Father promised
That He will give to you, but tarry in
Jerusalem and pray for power to do these things."

Lord, I want power to fulfill the Great Commission,
Give me supernatural results to my ministry.

During the 40 days since His death at Passover,
Jesus had been teaching His disciples
The things about God's plan for the Kingdom.
Jesus charged them to pray in Jerusalem after His departure
Until the Holy Spirit came upon them, even
As John the Baptist had promised, "You will be
Baptized with the Holy Spirit."
But the disciples asked, "Will You at this time usher
In the millennial kingdom and restore Israel as a
Sovereign nation?"
Jesus answered, "It is not for you to know the dates when
The Father will do all these things,
"But you will receive spiritual power when the Holy Spirit
Comes upon you, and you'll be My witnesses in
Jerusalem, Judea, Samaria, and throughout the whole world."

Then Jesus led them out of the city to the Mount of Olives,
He lifted His hands and blessed them.
While He was blessing them, Jesus was lifted into the heavens,
The disciples watched Him ascend into Heaven
And a cloud blocked their sight, so they saw Him no more.

The disciples continued staring into the sky until
> Two angels in white robes stood by them saying,

"Why are you staring into the sky? Jesus will
> Come again just as you have seen Him go."

The disciples worshiped Jesus and returned into the city
> With abundant joy, where they waited in prayer

> As Jesus had commanded them.

When Jesus returned to Heaven, He ascended the heights
> To sit down at the right hand of God, the Father.

Lord, because You're in Heaven as my intercessor,
> *I come to the Father through Your prayers.*

> *I am as close to the Father as You are to the heart of God.*

The Sixth Sunday After Pentecost

Acts 1:13-26

(See next volume—*Praying the Book of Acts*—of the series *Praying the Scripture* for a transliteration of the sixth and seventh Lord's Days after Pentecost. The following is a summary of what happened on the sixth and seventh Sundays after Pentecost.)

There were approximately 120 praying constantly in the Upper Room, doing exactly what Jesus commanded. He said, "I will return," so they probably expected Him on this Sunday, but Jesus didn't come, and the Holy Spirit didn't come. So, they examined themselves to see what else they had to do to be in the perfect will of God. Since the number eleven was a foreign number to Jews, and there were only eleven disciples, they decided to complete their number to twelve. They elected Matthias who had followed Jesus since John the Baptist had preached and he had seen a physical resurrection appearance of Jesus. I believe they should have waited for Paul, an apostle born out of due season.

The Seventh Sunday After Pentecost

Acts 2:1-4

The Holy Spirit came on Pentecost (the Latin word for 50), 50 days after Passover. The disciples were still praying in the Upper Room on Sunday morning when the Holy Spirit was poured out on them in revival (revival means God's presence was manifested among them). There were three outward supernatural signs: (1) the followers of Jesus spoke in other languages, (2) there was the sound of a mighty rushing wind, and (3) cloven flames of fire came on them. After Pentecost, God's people were never the same again, the Church took the place of Israel, and the world was never the same again.

THE END OF THE PHYSICAL LIFE OF JESUS IS THE BEGINNING OF THE CHURCH.

The thrilling work of Jesus Christ continues in, *Praying the Book of Acts—* the next book in the series, *Praying the Scriptures.*

ABOUT THE AUTHOR

Dr. Elmer Towns is an author of popular and scholarly works, a seminar lecturer, and dedicated worker in Sunday school. He has written over 125 books, including several best sellers. In 1995 he won the coveted Gold Medallion Book Award for *The Names of the Holy Spirit*.

Dr. Elmer Towns also cofounded Liberty University with Jerry Falwell in 1971 and now serves as Dean of the B.R. Lakin School of Religion and as professor of Theology and New Testament.

Liberty University was founded in 1971 and is the fastest growing Christian university in America. Located in Lynchburg, Virginia, Liberty University is a private, coeducational, undergraduate and graduate institution offering 38 undergraduate and 15 graduate programs serving over 25,000 resident and external students (9,600 on campus). Individuals from all 50 states and more than 70 nations comprise the diverse student body. While the faculty and students vary greatly, the common denominator and driving force of Liberty University since its conception is love for Jesus Christ and the desire to make Him known to the entire world.

For more information about Liberty University, contact:

Liberty University
1971 University Boulevard
Lynchburg, VA 24502
Telephone 434-582-2000
E-mail: www.Liberty.edu

ALSO FROM ELMER TOWNS

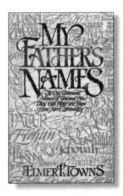

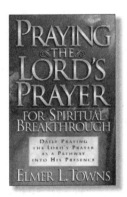
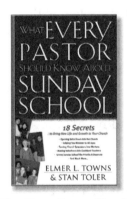

Praying the Psalms
To Touch God and
Be Touched by Him
Elmer Towns
ISBN: 0-7684-2195-0

Praying the Proverbs
Including Ecclesiastes and
the Song of Solomon
Elmer Towns
ISBN: 0-7684-2316-3

Praying the Book of Job
Learning How to Endure
Life's Hardships
Elmer Towns
ISBN: 0-7684-2361-9

Knowing God
Through Fasting
Foreword by Tommy Tenney
Elmer Towns
ISBN: 0-7684-2069-5

Personal Prayers